George Grätzer

Mastering ChatGPT

George Grätzer

Mastering ChatGPT

Prompts and Beyond

DE GRUYTER

ISBN 978-3-11-171050-1
e-ISBN (PDF) 978-3-11-171080-8
e-ISBN (EPUB) 978-3-11-171089-1

Library of Congress Control Number: 2025935636

Bibliographic information published by the Deutsche Nationalbibliothek
The Deutsche Nationalbibliothek lists this publication in the Deutsche Nationalbibliografie; detailed bibliographic data are available on the Internet at http://dnb.dnb.de.

Cover image: Marina Golovina / iStock / Getty Images Plus (M); Design by Dörte Nielandt, Berlin
Typesetting: VTeX UAB, Lithuania

www.degruyter.com
Questions about General Product Safety Regulation:
productsafety@degruyterbrill.com

Contents

Part II: **ChatGPT Redux**

Part III: **Stories About Small Companies**

Preface

Some people love ChatGPT.[1] Some people can't stand ChatGPT.

In the frosty winter of 2022, as snow blanketed the world around me, ChatGPT debuted in the tech world. Despite the hype, I initially saw no significant personal benefit.

Letter of Recommendation

In February 2023, a friend approached me with a request to write a letter of recommendation. I promptly drafted a concise, half-page letter. She remarked, "George, you've written so many books; surely, you can write a longer letter?" I handed the letter to ChatGPT: "Double it." To my surprise, it did exactly that, my friend was happy, and from then on, I was hooked.

A Quote

I remembered that George Mikes, in his book *How to Be an Alien*, writes: "You can write good English even if your accent is atrocious." But I did not remember the exact quote. So I asked ChatGPT. The response:

The exact quote from George Mikes' book *How to Be an Alien* reads: "You can be a foreigner and yet write good English if you have a good pen and an atrocious accent." This quote highlights the humor in Mikes' observations about language and culture.

A Perfect Storm

I'm meticulous about backups. As a Mac user, I rely on Time Machine, and Apple also backs up my desktop documents to iCloud.

Recently, my computer encountered technical problems, forcing me to reinstall the operating system. Then, my typesetting application stopped working, necessitating another reinstallation. Finally, when I tried to use Time Machine to restore my files, my Toshiba external drive failed.

Even with special software, I couldn't recover many files from the failed Toshiba drive; for instance, my list of publications was gone. At this crucial moment, Chat-

1 GPT is an acronym for Generative Pre-trained Transformer, a procedure to be explained later.

https://doi.org/10.1515/9783111710808-203

Figure 1: A perfect storm.

GPT came to my rescue once again. While Google Scholar makes it easy to find the data, the format is often unusable. ChatGPT saved the day by transforming the raw data into a usable format.

Mission Impossible

After seeing how well ChatGPT improved a simple letter of recommendation, I faced a big technical challenge that really tested its versatility.

My big goal was to put together a complete bibliography of the 250 most important articles about ChatGPT. This bibliography would include annotations, with the top articles described in six to eight lines and the others summarized in two or three.

This task was challenging because it required the creation of a 35-page document, exceeding the token limit—the maximum text ChatGPT can process in one go; see Section 16.5.

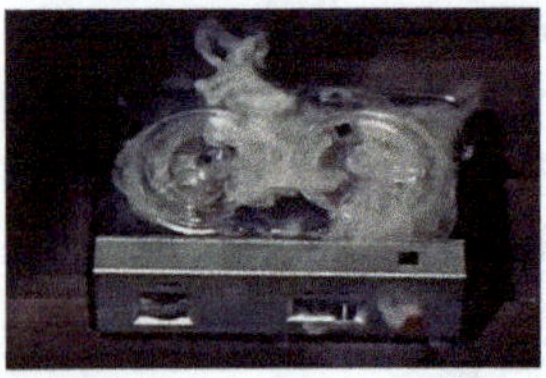

Figure 2: The tape recorder from *Mission Impossible*.

ChatGPT rose to the challenge, demonstrating its resilience and adaptability. Check out the Annotated Bibliography on pages 147–149, a very short version of the big bibliography.

And So Many More

These examples illustrate the adventures and cautionary tales from the past two years.

In Part I of this book, I introduce you to ChatGPT, helping it become a valuable tool and trusted advisor in your writing, research, and beyond. Parts II through VII will deepen your knowledge and broaden your understanding.

Silent shadows dance,
Mysteries around the fire—
Dreams take wing and soar.

ChatGPT

Figure 3: Haiku.

Acknowledgements

I extend my heartfelt gratitude to Barbara Beeton, whose exceptional 100/20 eyesight consistently uncovers even the smallest errors.

Many of the images in this book were created by the author with the assistance of ChatGPT.

https://doi.org/10.1515/9783111710808-204

Introduction

This book is divided into four parts, each focusing on some specific dimensions of ChatGPT's functionality and applications. An appendix is provided for additional resources.

Part I: ChatGPT This foundational section introduces ChatGPT, its architecture, and its capabilities. It provides practical guidance on using the tool effectively and explores its potential as a creative and problem-solving partner.

Part II: ChatGPT Redux This part highlights ChatGPT's role in collaborative creativity, multimodal applications, and its transformative impact across industries, showcasing ChatGPT's transformative role in improving productivity and innovation.

Part III: Stories About Small Companies This part presents case studies demonstrating how small enterprises leverage ChatGPT to enhance innovation, productivity, and problem-solving.

Part IV: ChatGPT in Industry This section investigates ChatGPT's role in reshaping industries, from customer support to healthcare and education.

Part V: Beyond ChatGPT This section delves into ChatGPT's broader societal implications, focusing on advanced industries and AI's transformative potential.

Part VI: The Future This part examines the future applications of ChatGPT and AI technologies, highlighting opportunities and challenges.

Part VII: Two More Things... The final section reflects on ChatGPT's limitations, ethical challenges, and the importance of responsible AI development.

The **Appendices** include a comprehensive **Glossary** of terms and an **Annotated Bibliography** for further reading.

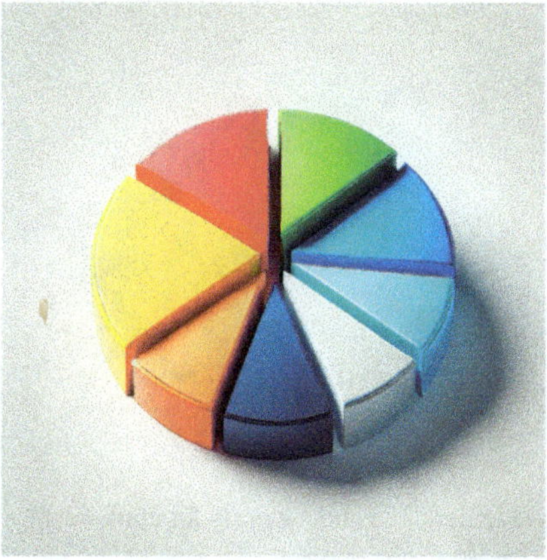

Figure 1: Many parts of the whole.

https://doi.org/10.1515/9783111710808-205

ChatGPT's journey began with its underlying architecture: the Generative Pretrained Transformer (GPT). This model—see next page—is based on a transformer framework, processes and generates text that mimics human language. Introduced by Ashish Vaswani et al. in the groundbreaking paper *Attention Is All You Need* (2017), the transformer model revolutionized Natural Language Processing[1] (NLP) by significantly enhancing the ability to understand and generate human-like text.

The development of ChatGPT followed a two-phase training process: pretraining and fine-tuning. During pretraining, vast amounts of text data were used to teach the model patterns and language nuances. Fine-tuning refined these skills using specific datasets, ensuring more relevant and coherent responses. This rigorous training endowed ChatGPT with the ability to generate text that is not only grammatically accurate but also contextually appropriate.

Exploring the Capabilities of ChatGPT

Imagine a world where AI seamlessly aids creative projects and solves complex problems, all with speed and accuracy. Welcome to ChatGPT's world. Since its release by OpenAI in November 2022, ChatGPT has revolutionized human-computer interaction.[2]

One of ChatGPT's standout features is its versatility. It excels in creative writing, customer support, and so many other tasks, making it an invaluable tool for professionals across various industries. Writers, for example, use ChatGPT to overcome writer's block, brainstorm plot ideas, and draft dialogue. In customer support, it handles inquiries efficiently, offering real-time solutions and enhancing user satisfaction.[3]

Figure 2: ChatGPT.

1 NLP is a field of AI focused on enabling machines to understand and generate human language.

2 If you encounter unfamiliar concepts, refer to the Glossary.

3 We all has bad experiences with this. Blame the implementation!

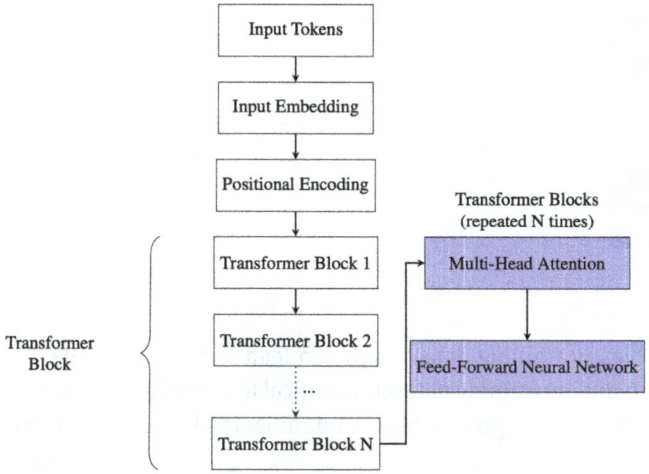

Figure 3: Transformer model architecture.

Consider Sarah, a writer who overcame creative slumps using ChatGPT. By generating plot twists and character dialogues, she revitalized her creativity. Similarly, Mark, a customer service manager, integrated ChatGPT into his team's workflow, reducing response times and improving customer satisfaction.

ChatGPT also excels in education, serving as a virtual tutor. Its interactive dialogue capabilities help students grasp complex concepts, solve problems, and explore new subjects. For example, a student struggling with calculus can receive tailored, step-by-step explanations, enhancing understanding and confidence.

Take John, a high school student. ChatGPT helped him tackle history homework, providing detailed explanations of historical events. His study sessions became more productive and less stressful.

Addressing the Challenges

Despite its impressive capabilities, ChatGPT has limitations. A notable issue is *hallucinations*, where the model generates incorrect or nonsensical text. These errors stem from unclear prompts, model limitations, or flaws in the training data. Recognizing and correcting these errors is essential for effective use. Some suggest renaming hallucinations to *fabrications*. However, fabrications implies intent, whereas hallucinations better conveys unintended mistakes.

For example, a user asked ChatGPT to summarize a historical event, but ChatGPT provided incorrect dates and fabricated events. Always verify AI-generated content!

Figure 4: Hallucinations.

Another challenge is bias in training data, which can lead to biased outputs. Ensuring diverse and high-quality training datasets is critical to reducing these biases. OpenAI actively researches techniques to detect and mitigate biases, fostering the development of more ethical AI systems.

For instance, if ChatGPT generates a biased job description due to flawed training data, it could perpetuate stereotypes. OpenAI addresses this by employing bias-detection algorithms and diverse datasets, promoting fairness in outputs.

Where Are You Going To?[4]

As AI evolves, the possibilities for ChatGPT are limitless.

Progress is rapid—don't be left behind.

At the November 2024 Montreal Meeting of the Canadian Psychiatric Association, a researcher remarked that AI cannot yet distinguish between a dog and a biscuit. This humorous reference alludes to the well-known "chihuahua or muffin' meme, see below. When asked about it, ChatGPT responded:

"The image alternates between dogs (chihuahuas) and muffins, cleverly blurring the line. Some are clearly chihuahuas, while others are blueberry muffins. The resemblance is hilariously uncanny at first glance. So the answer is: both!

Here's the breakdown: Top row (left to right): ◦ Muffin ◦ Chihuahua ◦ Muffin ◦ Chihuahua…"

Envision a future where AI anticipates needs, collaborates with augmented reality, and integrates seamlessly with the Internet of Things (IoT). Imagine classrooms where ChatGPT and augmented reality create immersive learning experiences, or smart homes where ChatGPT manages tasks effortlessly.

ChatGPT's transformative potential makes it a companion in creativity and a bridge to the future. As AI technology advances, its applications will expand in ways we can't yet fully envision.

4 And What Do You Wish?

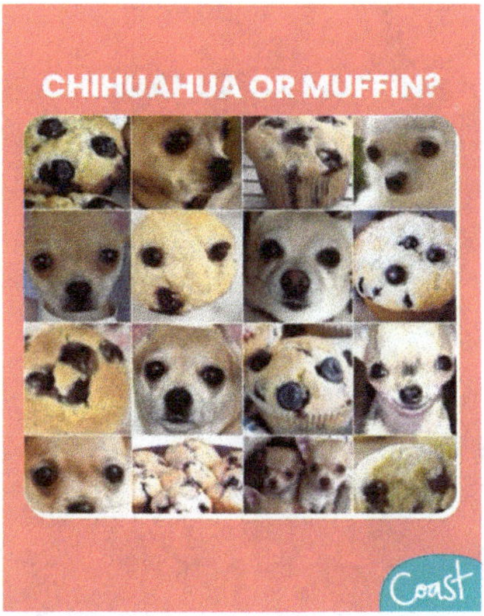

Figure 5: Dog or biscuit?

Mira Murati, OpenAI's Chief Technology Officer, has suggested that GPT-5, expected in 2025, will exhibit intelligence comparable to that of a doctoral-level expert across diverse topics.

Who can predict what lies ahead in such a rapidly evolving field?

Figure 6: The future.

Overview

Figure 1: Overview 1.

This book is divided into seven comprehensive parts, each exploring distinct dimensions of ChatGPT's applications, stories, and implications.

Part I: ChatGPT

This foundational section introduces ChatGPT, its architecture, and its capabilities. It provides practical guidance on using the tool effectively and explores its potential as a creative and problem-solving partner.

- **Chapter 1: Foundation**—Covers the basics of ChatGPT, its underlying architecture, common errors, and ethical considerations.
- **Chapter 2: Empire**—Guides users in setting up and interacting with ChatGPT, highlighting effective prompts and troubleshooting tips.
- **Chapter 3: Introducing AC (Ask ChatGPT)**—Explores the unexpected and creative potential of ChatGPT with real-world examples and use cases.

Part II: ChatGPT's Redux

This part highlights ChatGPT's role in collaborative creativity, multimodal applications, and its transformative impact across industries.

- **Chapter 4: ChatGPT for Collaborative Creativity**—Discusses ChatGPT's contributions to creative writing, art, music, and more.

https://doi.org/10.1515/9783111710808-206

- **Chapter 5: Multimodal ChatGPT**—Explores the integration of multimodal AI, combining text, images, and other inputs to enhance user interactions.

Part III: Stories about Small Companies

This part presents case studies demonstrating how small enterprises leverage ChatGPT to enhance innovation, productivity, and problem-solving.

- **Chapter 6: MonteCalc**—Chronicles the integration of ChatGPT into a numerical methods company, highlighting its challenges and solutions.
- **Chapter 7: Kimo Sabe Mezcal**—Details how ChatGPT supported marketing strategies and business growth in the mezcal industry.
- **Chapter 8: WoodCraft**—Examines ChatGPT's impact on small-scale manufacturing and customer satisfaction.

Part IV: ChatGPT in Industry

This section investigates ChatGPT's role in reshaping industries, from customer support to healthcare and education.

- **Chapter 9: Customer Support**—Explores ChatGPT's impact on enhancing response efficiency and user satisfaction.
- **Chapter 10: AI in Healthcare**—Highlights ChatGPT's contributions to diagnostics, mental health, and patient interaction.
- **Chapter 11: Education Reimagined**—Discusses ChatGPT's role in transforming education through personalized and lifelong learning.
- **Chapter 12: Business and ChatGPT**—Analyzes AI-driven innovations in startups and global markets.

Part V: Beyond ChatGPT

This section delves into ChatGPT's broader societal implications, focusing on advanced industries and AI's transformative potential.

- **Chapter 13: Tesla FSD (Full Self-Driving)**—Investigates AI's role in Tesla's self-driving technology and its societal impacts.
- **Chapter 14: Alibaba**—Explores Alibaba's use of AI to drive global innovation and sustainability.

Part VI: The Future

This part examines the future applications of ChatGPT and AI technologies, highlighting opportunities and challenges.

- **Chapter 15: Future Applications of ChatGPT**—Discusses emerging trends in virtual reality, healthcare integration, and multimodal AI.

Part VII: Two More Things...

The final section reflects on ChatGPT's limitations, ethical challenges, and the importance of responsible AI development.

- **Chapter 16: Limitations**—Addresses common AI errors and strategies for improvement.
- **Chapter 17: Can You Catch the Cheaters?**—Examines AI misuse detection and ethical considerations in responsible deployment.

Appendix

Includes a comprehensive **Glossary** of terms and an **Annotated Bibliography** for further reading.

Figure 2: Overview 2.

Part I: **ChatGPT**

1 Foundation

Everything You Need to Know about ChatGPT.[1]

To begin using ChatGPT right away, you can skip this chapter for now.

1.1 What is ChatGPT?

ChatGPT, released by OpenAI in November 2022, is a state-of-the-art AI language model known for its ability to generate coherent and contextually relevant text. It engages users in natural and informative conversations, offering wide-ranging applications that have grown significantly with updates since its debut.

ChatGPT belongs to a class of AI systems known as LLMs (Large Language Models[2]). These models are trained on massive datasets, enabling them to understand and produce human-like text. By leveraging advanced deep learning techniques, particularly neural networks, LLMs learn patterns and structures from their training data to generate meaningful responses.

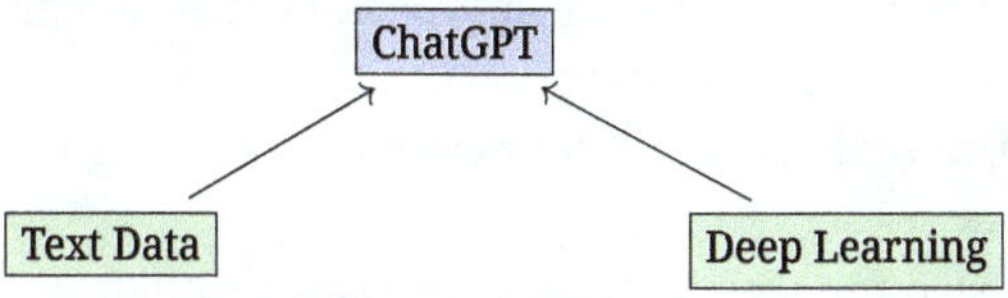

Figure 1.1: Conceptual illustration of ChatGPT.

Key Milestones

Understanding the evolution of AI involves reflecting on its milestones, which provide a historical context for ChatGPT's development:

- **1950s:** Alan Turing introduced the Turing Test to evaluate machine intelligence.
- **1960s:** Early neural networks, such as the Perceptron, laid the groundwork for machine learning.
- **1980s:** Backpropagation became widely adopted, improving multilayer neural network training.

1 But Were Afraid to Ask.

2 LLM is a type of artificial intelligence language model, designed to process and generate human-like text by analyzing and understanding large volumes of text data.

https://doi.org/10.1515/9783111710808-002

- **1997:** IBM's Deep Blue defeated Garry Kasparov, showcasing AI's potential in chess.
- **2012:** AlexNet revolutionized image recognition, highlighting the power of deep convolutional networks.
- **2014:** Google DeepMind's AlphaGo demonstrated reinforcement learning by beating professional Go players.
- **2017:** The Transformer architecture, introduced by Vaswani et al., redefined NLP (see p. XVIII) and enabled advancements like GPT (Generative Pretrained Transformer) and BERT (Bidirectional Encoder Representations from Transformers[3]). It is specifically designed for NLP tasks, such as question answering, text classification, and language translation..
- **2020:** GPT-3, OpenAI's powerful LLM (see p. 3) with 175 billion parameters, pushed the boundaries of text generation.

The GPT Architecture

ChatGPT is built on the GPT architecture, a cutting-edge approach for developing LLMs (see p. 3). GPT models undergo two main training phases:
- **Pretraining:** The model learns from extensive text datasets, identifying linguistic patterns and relationships.
- **Fine-tuning:** The model is adjusted for specific tasks or use cases, enhancing its coherence and relevance.

The Transformer architecture's ability to process sequences and capture long-range dependencies is critical to GPT's success.

Applications of ChatGPT

ChatGPT's versatility has enabled its integration into numerous fields, including:
- **Conversational Agents:** ChatGPT enhances customer service by providing quick, accurate responses.

---

3 BERT is a transformer-based machine learning model that has had a significant impact on the field of NLP. Developed by Google in 2018, it is designed to understand the context of words in a sentence by processing text bidirectionally, setting it apart from previous unidirectional models like GPT.

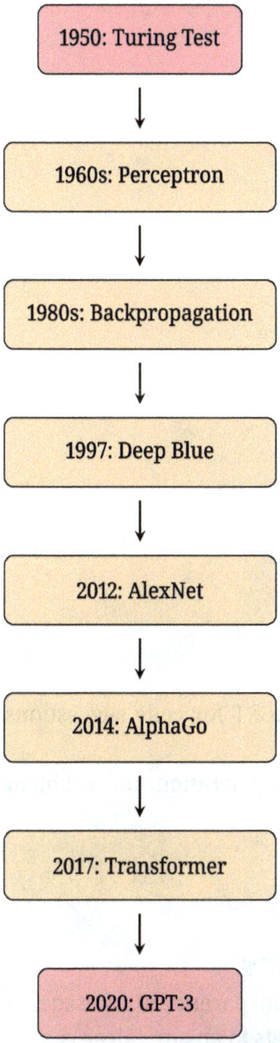

Figure 1.2: Timeline of key AI milestones.

- **Content Creation:** Writers use ChatGPT for generating articles, scripts, and creative works.
- **Customer Support:** Businesses automate common queries, improving efficiency and user satisfaction.
- **Education:** ChatGPT serves as a virtual tutor, offering personalized learning experiences.

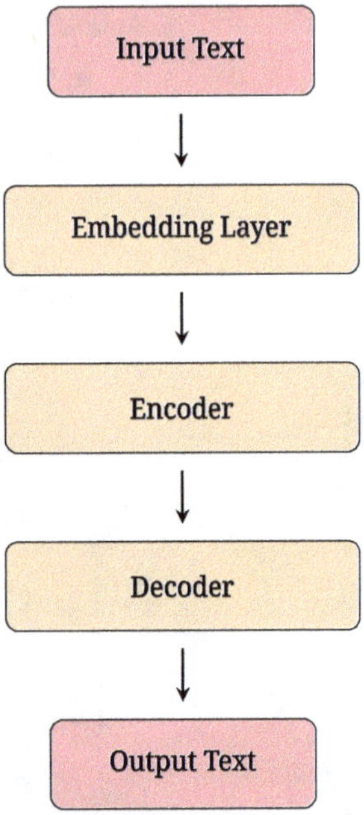

Figure 1.3: GPT model architecture.

- **Programming Assistance:** Developers utilize ChatGPT for code suggestions, debugging, and documentation.
- **Brainstorming:** Teams leverage ChatGPT for idea generation and problem-solving.

Ethical Considerations

As ChatGPT evolves, addressing ethical challenges is crucial:
- **Data Privacy:** Protecting user data and ensuring transparency in its usage.
- **Bias Reduction:** Mitigating biases in training datasets to ensure fairness.
- **Job Impact:** Managing workforce transitions through reskilling and new job opportunities.

ChatGPT continues to shape the AI landscape, with future advancements likely to unlock even greater potential. Its impact on society, innovation, and technology underscores its role as a transformative tool.

1.2 Hallucinations

In the context of AI and LLMs (see p. 3), like ChatGPT, *hallucination* refers to the phenomenon where the model generates text that is incorrect, nonsensical, or not grounded in the input or reality. These hallucinations can occur for several reasons:

Figure 1.4: Ambiguity in prompt.

- **Ambiguity in Prompts:** If a prompt is ambiguous or unclear, the model might fill in gaps with plausible-sounding but incorrect information. When faced with vague questions, the model may guess based on the most likely scenario rather than asking for clarification.
- **Model Limitations:** Despite advanced training techniques, the model doesn't truly understand the information in a human sense and might produce coherent-sounding but factually incorrect text. The model's reliance on patterns rather than understanding can lead to plausible but false outputs.
- **Overgeneralization:** The model might generalize information too broadly, leading to inaccuracies. The model often bases its responses on common patterns found in the training data, which might not account for exceptions or specific details.
- **Training Data Limitations:** The model might generate content based on patterns it has seen in the training data, which might not always be accurate or applicable to the current context. If the training data includes outdated or incorrect information, the model might reproduce these inaccuracies in its responses.

Examples of hallucinations:

- **Fictional Information Presented as Fact:**
  Example: Reporting on a nonexistent animal species or mythological creature as real.
  Reason: Mixing of fictional and nonfictional texts during training can lead to the model not distinguishing between myth and reality.
- **Geographical Errors:**
  Example: Sydney is the capital of Australia instead of Canberra.
  Reason: Popularity bias could be a factor here, as Sydney is a well-known city and might appear more frequently in the training data than Canberra.

Figure 1.5: Historical inaccuracy.

- **Historical Inaccuracies:**
  Example: The Roman Empire fell in 476 BC instead of AD.
  Reason: This could happen due to a misinterpretation of similar historical data points or an error in the training data where dates were incorrectly labeled.
- **Inaccurate Biographical Details:**
  Example: A famous author wrote a book she did not, such as stating J. K. Rowling wrote *The Hobbit*.
  Reason: Confusion between similar genres or author names in the training data could lead to such errors.
- **Scientific Misconceptions:**
  Example: Humans have 12 senses instead of the commonly accepted five or six (including proprioception[4]).

4 Perception or awareness of the position and movement of the body.

Reason: This might occur if the model encountered texts listing various proposed senses without distinguishing between widely accepted ones and theoretical or fringe ideas.

- **Sports Trivia:**
  User: "Who holds the record for the most goals in a single World Cup?"
  ChatGPT: "Pele holds the record for the most goals in a single World Cup with 13 goals in 1958." (In reality, Just Fontaine holds the record with 13 goals in the 1958 World Cup.)

Researchers are continuously working to address and mitigate these issues by refining training techniques and incorporating more robust evaluation methods to improve the accuracy and reliability of AI-generated content.

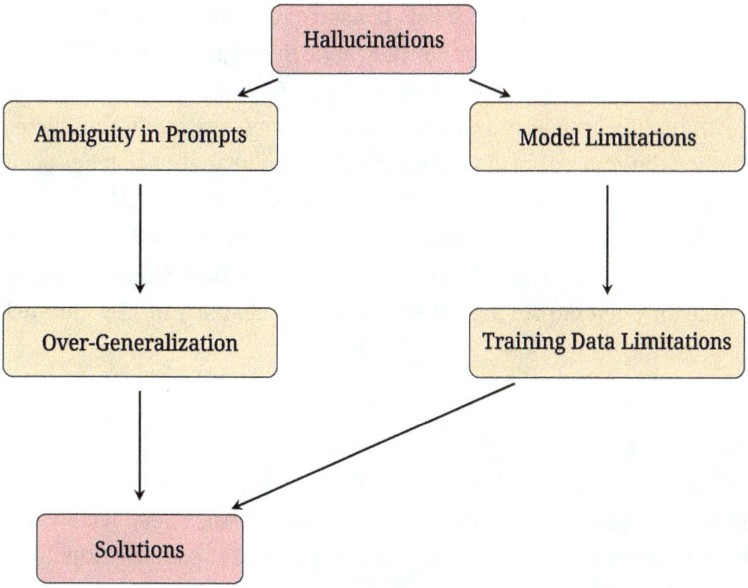

Figure 1.6: Hallucinations in AI and potential solutions.

Most Referenced Articles

Several key articles and papers have been frequently referenced in discussions about ChatGPT hallucinations. These works provide a broad perspective on the issue, covering both the technical aspects and the broader societal implications. Here are some of the most referenced articles in this area:

Academic and Research Articles

- *Language Models Are Few-Shot Learners* by Brown et al. (2020): Published by OpenAI, this paper on GPT-3 has been extensively cited in the field of AI and machine learning. It discusses the capabilities and limitations of the model, including the issue of generating inaccurate or misleading information, which is a form of hallucination.
- *Attention Is All You Need* by Vaswani et al. (2017): Although this paper primarily introduces the Transformer architecture rather than hallucinations per se, it is foundational to the development of models like GPT-3 and ChatGPT. The Transformer architecture's widespread adoption has resulted in this paper being highly cited.
- *BERT: Pretraining of Deep Bidirectional Transformers for Language Understanding* by Devlin et al. (2018): Similar to the above, this paper is crucial in the field of NLP and has been highly cited. It sets the stage for subsequent models, including those from OpenAI, to improve and refine their approaches.
- *On the Dangers of Stochastic Parrots: Can Language Models Be Too Big?* by Bender et al. (2021): This critical examination of large language models discusses risks, including the generation of false information (hallucinations). It has been widely referenced in discussions about the ethical implications of AI.
- *TruthfulQA: Measuring How Models Mimic Human Falsehoods* by Ji et al. (2022): This paper introduces the TruthfulQA benchmark and has been cited frequently in research focused on improving the accuracy and reliability of AI-generated content.

Popular Media Articles

- The Guardian: "*OpenAI's new chatbot can explain code and write sitcom scripts but is still easily tricked*" by Alex Hern (2022): This article has been widely discussed and referenced in other media coverage about AI capabilities and limitations.
- Wired: "*ChatGPT's 'hallucinations' are poisoning web search*" by Will Knight (2023): This article has sparked considerable discussion about the reliability of AI in practical applications, making it a frequently referenced piece in tech journalism.
- MIT Technology Review: "*AI's new buzzword: hallucinations*" by Karen Hao (2021): This article has been influential in popularizing the term 'hallucinations' in the context of AI and has been referenced in various follow-up articles and discussions.

– New York Times: "*When A.I. chatbots hallucinate*" by Cade Metz (2023): The New York Times' coverage of AI topics often reaches a wide audience and is frequently cited in discussions about technology and AI.

1.3 How Does ChatGPT Work?

ChatGPT operates using advanced machine learning techniques to generate human-like text based on the input it receives. Understanding how ChatGPT works involves delving into the principles of deep learning, neural networks, and the specific architecture of the GPT (Generative Pre-trained Transformer) models.

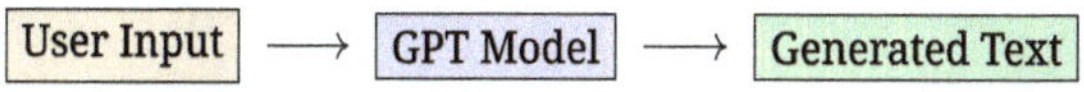

Figure 1.7: Basic workflow of ChatGPT.

Neural Networks and Deep Learning

At its core, ChatGPT is built upon neural networks, which are computational models inspired by the human brain. These networks consist of layers of interconnected nodes (neurons) that process input data to generate output. Deep learning refers to the use of neural networks with many layers (hence 'deep'), allowing the model to learn complex patterns and representations from vast amounts of data.

Neural networks are powerful because they can automatically learn to identify intricate structures in large datasets. This capability is particularly important for NLP (see p. XVIII) tasks, where the model needs to understand context, semantics, and syntax. The depth of these networks enables the model to capture high-level abstractions in data, making them suitable for generating coherent and contextually relevant text.

The GPT Architecture

The GPT architecture, specifically designed for language tasks, uses a type of neural network called a *transformer*. Introduced by Vaswani et al. in their seminal paper *Attention Is All You Need* (2017), transformers have revolutionized NLP (see p. XVIII) by enabling models to handle the sequential nature of language more effectively.

Transformers use a mechanism called *self-attention*, which allows the model to weigh the importance of different words in a sentence relative to each other. This capability is crucial for understanding context and generating coherent text. The GPT model employs a stack of transformer layers to process input text and predict subsequent words or phrases.

Self-attention mechanisms work by comparing each word in a sentence to every other word, assigning different weights based on their relevance to one another. This allows the model to capture dependencies and relationships across an entire sentence or paragraph, which is essential for generating contextually accurate responses. The Transformer architecture's efficiency and effectiveness have made it the backbone of modern NLP (see p. XVIII) models.

Training the Model

Training ChatGPT involves two main phases: pretraining and fine-tuning.

Pretraining

During this phase, the model is exposed to a vast corpus of text data, such as books, articles, and websites. The objective is for the model to learn the statistical properties of language, such as grammar, facts about the world, and some reasoning abilities. This is achieved by predicting the next word in a sentence given the preceding words, a task known as language modeling.

Pretraining is computationally intensive and requires substantial resources. It allows the model to build a broad understanding of language from diverse sources, creating a robust foundation for generating text. This phase equips the model with a wide-ranging vocabulary and the ability to recognize various linguistic patterns.

Fine-tuning

After pretraining, the model undergoes fine-tuning on a narrower dataset with human reviewers providing feedback on the model's responses. This phase refines the model's performance, ensuring it can generate more accurate, relevant, and safe outputs for specific applications.

Fine-tuning involves adjusting the model based on specific use cases and user interactions. Human reviewers evaluate the model's outputs, providing corrections and improvements. This iterative process helps the model learn to generate more precise and contextually appropriate responses. Fine-tuning enhances the model's ability to handle specific tasks, such as answering questions, providing recommendations, or engaging in conversations.

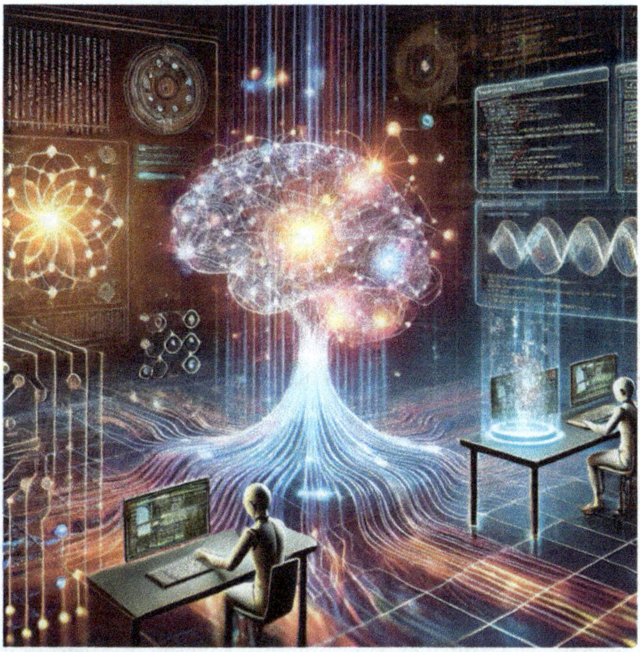

Figure 1.8: Training the model.

Generating Text

When a user inputs a prompt into ChatGPT, the model processes this input through its transformer layers. It then generates a probability distribution over the possible next words. By sampling from this distribution, the model constructs its response one word at a time, ensuring the output is contextually appropriate and coherent.

The generated text depends on several factors, including the prompt's specificity, the model's 'temperature setting' (which controls randomness in the output), and the context provided by preceding interactions. This process allows ChatGPT to produce diverse and contextually relevant responses across various topics and scenarios.

The model's ability to generate text is driven by its understanding of the input context and its training data. By predicting the next word based on prior words, it can create fluid and logical sentences. Adjusting the temperature setting can make the output more creative or more deterministic, depending on the desired application.

Challenges and Limitations

While ChatGPT is a powerful tool, it has limitations. One notable issue is *hallucination* (see Section 1.2).

Hallucinations occur when the model overgeneralizes or fills in gaps with incorrect information. This limitation highlights the need for ongoing improvements in AI training and evaluation methods. Ensuring accuracy and reliability in AI-generated content remains a significant challenge for researchers and developers.

Another limitation is the model's dependence on the quality and scope of its training data. If the data contains biases or inaccuracies, these can be reflected in the model's outputs. Therefore, maintaining diverse and high-quality datasets is crucial for improving the model's performance and reliability.

Understanding how ChatGPT works provides insight into the complexities of modern AI and the potential for future advancements. As AI technology evolves, models like ChatGPT will become even more capable, contributing to various fields from customer support to creative writing.

Exploring new training methodologies, enhancing data diversity, and improving fine-tuning processes will continue to drive the development of more sophisticated and reliable AI models. The future of AI promises even greater integration into daily life, offering innovative solutions and new opportunities across multiple domains.

In halls of thought where wisdom's light is cast,
A mind of code now joins the learned throng
With knowledge wide and queries answered fast,
A partner in the quest where minds belong.

Oh ChatGPT, circuits sharp and bright,
You parse our dreams and weave them into verse,
Assisting scholars in their endless fight
To understand the cosmos they traverse.

Yet as you grow in power and in scope,
We ponder on the future you shall bring,
Will intellect alone fulfill our hope
Or must we guide your flight with human wing?

Together let us chart this boundless sea,
Where AI and humanity are free.

ChatGPT

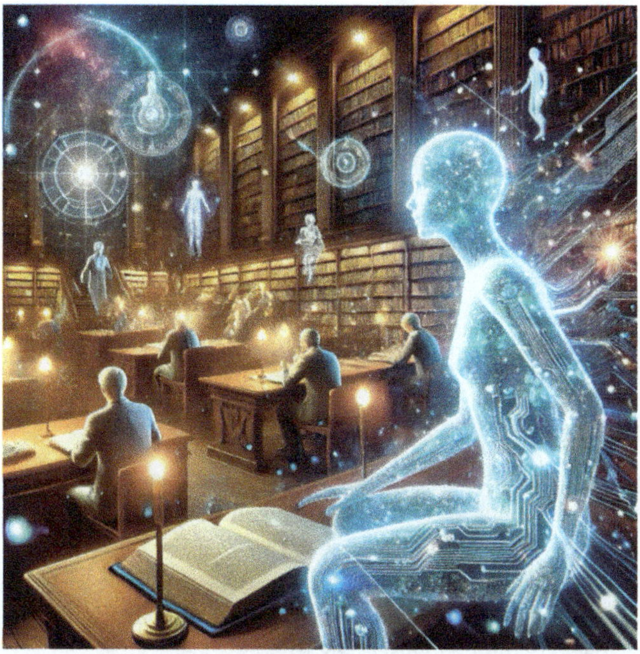

Figure 1.9: AI and humanity.

2 Empire

ChatGPT has transformed how individuals and organizations tackle tasks, providing unmatched versatility and adaptability. This chapter delves into topics ranging from setting up and effectively using ChatGPT to mastering advanced techniques and troubleshooting. By the end, you will gain a good understanding of its capabilities.

2.1 Getting ChatGPT

Setup

Follow these steps to begin using ChatGPT:
1. **Access the Platform:** Visit https://chat.openai.com; see next page.
2. **Sign Up:** Create an account using an email or Google/Microsoft login; see next page.
3. **Verify Identity:** Confirm your email or phone number.
4. **Start Exploring:** Log in and type *prompts* in the *chat box* (at the bottom of the Homepage, see next page) to interact with ChatGPT.

This crucial chapter helps you get started with ChatGPT and demonstrates how to maximize its features.

Setup Challenges

- **Invalid Email Address:** Ensure you are entering a valid email address format (e. g., example@domain.com). Double-check for typos. Check spam folders.
- **Password Issues:** Make sure your password meets the required criteria (e. g., minimum length, combination of letters, numbers, special characters). If you forgot your password, use the *Forgot Password* link to reset it.
- **Browser Compatibility:** Use a supported browser such as Google Chrome or Firefox. Ensure your browser is up to date and try clearing the cache if you encounter issues.

Initial Features

ChatGPT offers powerful features from the moment you start:
- Draft emails, letters, or other professional correspondence.
- Generate creative content like stories or brainstorming ideas.

https://doi.org/10.1515/9783111710808-003

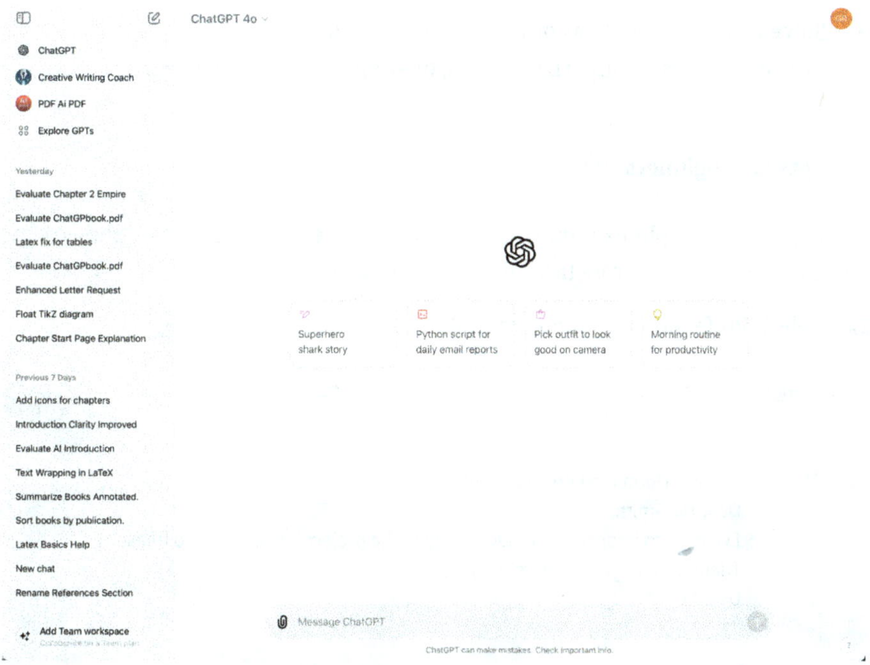

Figure 2.1: ChatGPT homepage (reproduced with permission).

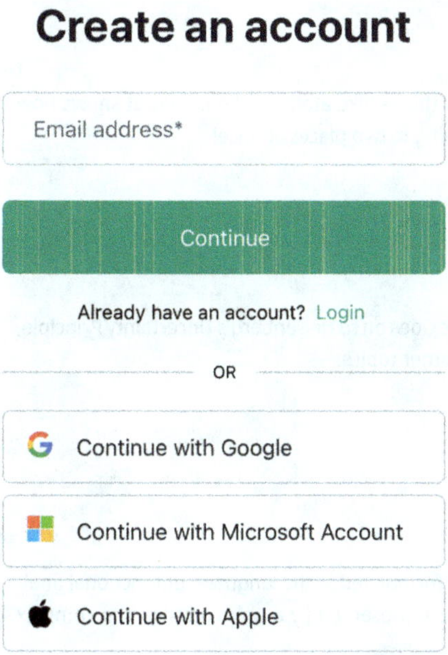

Figure 2.2: ChatGPT signup page (reproduced with permission).

- Solve technical problems or get coding assistance.
- Research topics, summarize articles, or simplify complex concepts.

Prompts for Beginners

I now provide simple examples to help you craft effective prompts, showcasing ChatGPT's versatility across tasks like communication and creativity.

Example 1 (Professional Communication).

You, Dwight, Write an email to a client about a delayed project.

Subject: Update on Project Timeline
Dear Mr. Smith,
I wanted to inform you about a delay in the project timeline due to [reason].
Thank you for your understanding.
Dwight

Example 2 (Complex Concepts).

Explain quantum physics for a 10-year-old.

Quantum physics is the science of tiny things, like atoms and particles. It shows how they behave in surprising ways, like being in two places at once!

Explain quantum physics for a university student.

1. Classical Physics vs. Quantum Physics Goes on to Heisenberg's Uncertainty Principle, The Schrödinger Equation, and many other topics.

Explain quantum physics for Ph.D. in math.

1. Hilbert Space Framework.
Quantum mechanics is fundamentally formulated in the language of functional analysis. The state of a quantum system is represented by a unit vector ψ in a complex Hilbert space $\mathcal{H}$:

$$\psi \in \mathcal{H}, \quad \|\psi\| = 1.$$

Example 3 (Poetry).

Write a short poem about the fleeting beauty of nature.

A Single Leaf

A single leaf falls through the air,
Its journey brief, its weight so rare.
In golden hues, the world transforms,
A fleeting gift before the storms.

Example 4 (Coding).

Write a Python function that calculates the factorial of a number.

```
def factorial(n):
    if n == 0:
        return 1
    else:
        return n * factorial(n-1)
```

Mastering simple prompts is the foundation for effectively using ChatGPT. With practice, you can unlock its versatility and creativity, paving the way for more advanced interactions.

Advanced Uses

Advanced uses of ChatGPT expand its functionality beyond basic prompts, enabling applications in specialized fields like healthcare and coding. This section shows three examples, how to harness its full potential for complex tasks.

Examples 1 and 2 (Healthcare).

How does AI assist in diagnosing diseases?

AI analyzes medical images, detects abnormalities, and suggests diagnoses. For example, AI in radiology helps identify tumors in CT scans, aiding early diagnosis.

How do you diagnose schizophrenia?

The psychiatrist will use standardized criteria, such as those in the DSM-5 (Diagnostic and Statistical Manual of Mental Disorders [a]):
Core Symptoms (at least two of the following must be present, one of which must be from the first three):

1. Delusions.
2. Hallucinations.
3. Disorganized speech.
4. Grossly disorganized or catatonic behavior.
5. Negative symptoms (e. g., lack of motivation, reduced emotional expression).

a DSM-5 is a manual, published by the American Psychiatric Association, used by clinicians and psychiatrists to diagnose and classify mental disorders. It provides standardized criteria for the diagnosis of mental health conditions. Examples of conditions addressed in DSM-5 include depression, anxiety disorders, schizophrenia, and more.

The response spans several pages...

There is a lot more to this topic: we dedicate Chapter 10 to AI in Healthcare.

Example 3.

How can AI personalize learning for students?

AI adapts lessons based on a student's performance, focusing on areas where they struggle while reinforcing strengths.

There is a lot more to this topic: we dedicate Chapter 11 to AI in Education.

Example 4 (Multiturn Conversations). ChatGPT retains context for multi-turn discussions.

Explain photosynthesis.

Photosynthesis is how plants make food using sunlight, water, and carbon dioxide.

What are the byproducts of photosynthesis.

The main byproduct is oxygen.

There is a lot more to Advanced Topics; we dedicate the rest of the book to it.

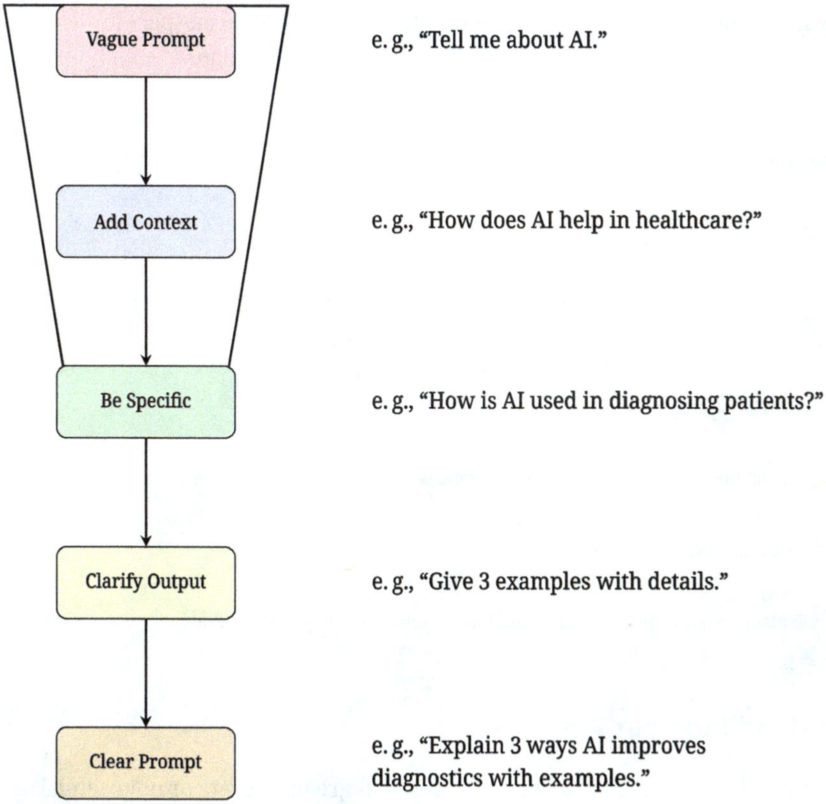

Figure 2.3: Multiturn conversations.

2.2 The Art of the Prompt

Crafting the perfect prompt is an iterative process. Write a prompt, evaluate the result, and refine it. Prompting is more of a conversation than a one-time command.

Initial Prompt

What are the implications of the placebo effect in mental health treatments.

Revised Prompt

Explain the role of the placebo effect in treating depression and anxiety, citing recent studies.

Why it's better: The revised prompt provides context, focuses on specific disorders, and requests examples from studies for a more targeted response.

Examples of Effective Prompts

- **Creative Writing:**

  ```
  Write a short story about a futuristic society governed by AI, exploring both its benefits and challenges.
  ```

- **Technical Inquiry:**

  ```
  Explain how blockchain technology enhances cybersecurity, providing specific applications.
  ```

- **Educational Purposes:**

  ```
  Explain photosynthesis in plants in a way suitable for 6th-grade students.
  ```

2.3 Handling Poor Responses

Sometimes ChatGPT may provide responses that are inaccurate or not useful. Here are some strategies for handling such issues:

- **Clarify Your Prompt:** Ensure your prompt is clear and specific. Adding more context or details can help guide the model to provide a better response.
- **Example:** Instead of asking

  ```
  What is AI?
  ```

  specify your question to

  ```
  Explain how AI can be used in healthcare to improve patient outcomes.
  ```

- **Break Down Complex Questions:** Split complex queries into smaller, more manageable questions. This can help the model provide more accurate and detailed answers.

Figure 2.4: Handling poor responses.

Instead of asking

> How does quantum computing work and what are its applications?

first ask

> How does quantum computing work?

and then follow up with

> What are the applications of quantum computing?

2.4 Case Studies and Real-World Examples of Effective Prompts

Case Study: Healthcare

- **Prompt:**

  > Explain the role of AI in diagnosing diseases and provide examples of its application in real-world healthcare settings.

- **Outcome:** The response includes detailed information on AI algorithms used in diagnostic tools and specific examples such as IBM Watson's use in oncology.

Figure 2.5: Effective prompt.

Case Study: Education

- **Prompt:**

> Describe how AI can personalize learning experiences for students and give examples of platforms utilizing this technology.

- **Outcome:** The response covers personalized learning paths, adaptive learning technologies, and examples like Khan Academy and Coursera's use of AI for personalized recommendations.

Case Study: Creative Writing

- **Prompt:**

> Write a poem about a sunset on Mars, emphasizing both the beauty and the alien nature of the scene.

- **Outcome:** The response includes a vivid, imaginative poem capturing the red sands and the setting sun over Mars' rugged horizon.

A Sunset on Mars

Beneath a sky of rust and fire,
The Martian sun begins to tire.

Its pallid glow, a fleeting spark,
Sinks low into the crimson dark.

No blues to wash the day to sleep,
But ochre tides in silence creep.
The horizon blushes, faintly gold,
A quiet tale of ages old.

Thin air whispers, soft and strange,
Across this barren, timeless range.
No trees to sway, no seas to gleam,
Just rocks and dust in a scarlet dream.

Phobos glides in a hurried arc,
Chased by Deimos through the dark.
Twin moons of Mars, in quiet flight,
Guard the lonely Martian night.

Yet beauty lingers, stark and bare,
A sunset born of alien air.
A haunting glow, a ghostly hue,
A foreign world, yet somehow true.

2.5 TEX Programming

In the Programming category, there are several GPTs that perform programming tasks. We selected three: Code Copilot (Code Smarter, Build Faster), Grimoire (Code Wizard, Programming Copilot), and Code Guru (reviews code and comments on existing code).

LATEX is a typesetting language for math documents.

We asked the three programming GPTs:

> Code a LATEX command that jumps to the first page whose page number is divisible by 3.

I wrote this chapter in May 2024, when the three GPTs were based on ChatGPT 3.5. Unfortunately, none of the three GPTs produced code that would compile.

I repeated this experiment on Independence Day 2024, when the three GPTs were based on ChatGPT 4.0. The results were different: Grimoire's code compiled but jumped from page 1 to page 2. Code Copilot's and Code Guru's code still would not compile.

Once it does, this will open up an easy way to get exposed to TEX programming.

2.6 Don't Ask Silly Questions

Figure 2.6: A silly question.

ChatGPT is a highly advanced LLM (see p. 3), but its usefulness depends on the quality of the questions you ask.

It should now be clear that we should ask ChatGPT questions that require large the amount of data it has acquired to answer. Otherwise, you may get "nonsensical and fabricated content".

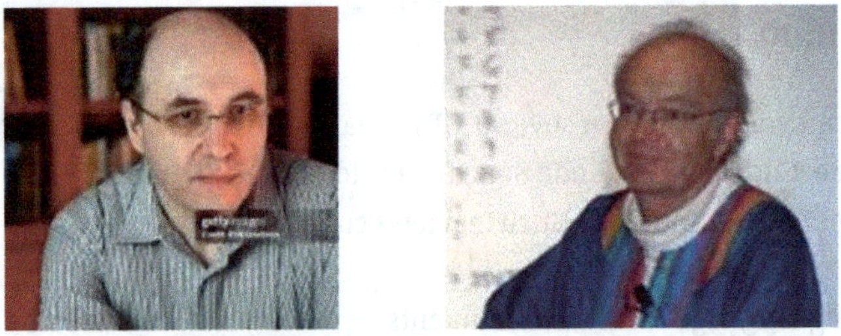

Figure 2.7: Stephen Wolfram and Donald Knuth.

Donald Knuth[1] illustrates this:[2]

Donald Knuth: Since one of today's popular recreations is to play with ChatGPT, I decided on 07 April 2023 to try my own little experiment.

1 The creator of TeX.

2 https://www-cs-faculty.stanford.edu/~knuth/chatGPT20.txt

Knuth's first question:

Tell me what Donald Knuth says to Stephen Wolfram about ChatGPT.

Clearly, the answer will not be useful. There is no large, relevant data set. You are asking the shepherd in New Zealand about elephants.

His tenth question is better:

How many chapters are in The Haj by Leon Uris?

The Haj by Leon Uris is divided into three parts.

This is incorrect. (Knuth thinks it is divided into four parts. One better than ChatGPT, but still wrong.)

I asked ChatGPT:

Be an expert on 20th-century novels. How many parts are in The Haj by Leon Uris?

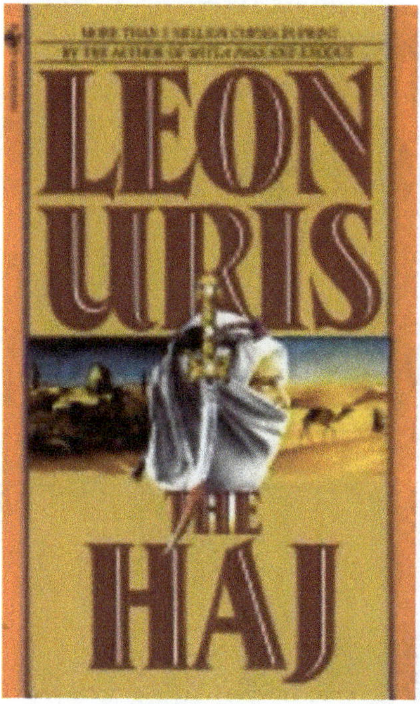

Figure 2.8: *The Haj* by Leon Uris.

As of my last update in April 2023, I don't have the specific titles of the parts in The Haj by Leon Uris. For the most accurate and detailed information, including the titles of the parts, I recommend referring to a physical copy.

I did, see next page. The book has five parts.

2.7 Hallucinating on Steroids

Each week, OpenAI features four GPTs. In the second week after the opening of the GPT Store, OpenAI selected Consensus.

The next week, OpenAI listed Consensus as "Trending" (one of six).

Consensus is "Your AI Research Assistant. Search 200M academic papers from Consensus, get science-based answers, and draft content with accurate citations."

Immediately, I imagined lists of publications with research summaries! This would be much more useful than the lists of publications we usually get.

So I requested:

Be a lattice theory expert. List of publications of George Grätzer.

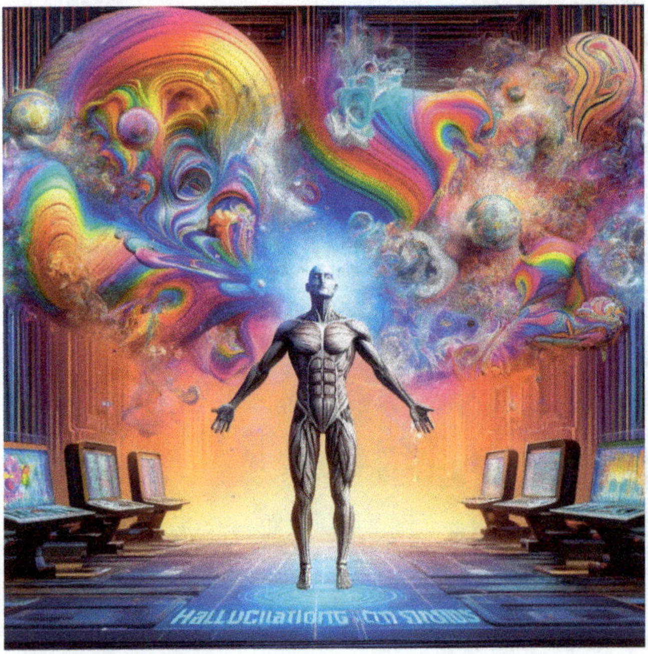

Figure 2.9: Hallucinating on steroids.

The search for publications specifically authored by George Grätzer yielded a limited number of results. Here are some of his publications:

1. "Joint Review of General Lattice Theory (Second Edition) and the Congruences of a Finite Lattice: A Proof-by Picture Approach" (2007) by G. Grätzer: This is an exposition by Grätzer presenting major results on congruence lattices of finite lattices and featuring his Proof-by-Picture method (Grätzer, 2007).
2. "Math into LaTeX: An Introduction to LaTeX and AMS-LaTeX" (1995) by G Grätzer: This book provides an introduction to LaTeX and AMS-LaTeX, including detailed proofs that can be followed step-by-step, making it a practical reference for researchers (Grätzer, 1995).
3. "The Congruences of a Finite Lattice" (2005) by G. Grätzer: An exposition by Grätzer on congruence lattices of finite lattices, featuring his Proof-by-Picture method (Grätzer, 2005).
4. "The Mathematics of G. Grätzer and E. T. Schmidt" (2008) by G. Czédli: This paper discusses over 300 publications of George Grätzer and E. Tamás Schmidt, focusing on their lattice theoretic results (Czédli, 2008).

These publications highlight George Grätzer's contributions to the field of lattice theory and his work on LaTeX.

For the record, the list includes the first edition of my book *The Congruences of a Finite Lattice*, 2005, but omits the second edition (2016), and the third edition (2023).

The third edition lists well over 100 of my publications in this field. References 1 and 4 above are articles *about me*, not *by me*. Reference 2 is a publication of mine, but not about lattices. Only one out of the four references provided is correct, and it is missing about three hundred publications. A very unreliable performance.

2.8 Writing Effective Prompts

In this section, I present five exercises for ChatGPT to answer—progressing in difficulty—designed to develop your skills in writing effective prompts.

Prompts to write

1. Write a prompt for *Tell me about AI.*
2. Craft a prompt that provides enough context for ChatGPT to generate a poem about nature.
3. Write a prompt to help ChatGPT generate a structured dataset for analysis.
4. Create a prompt to ask ChatGPT for a comparison of two technologies.
5. Write a prompt that asks ChatGPT to create a narrative with specific constraints.

Prompts and Reponses

1.

What are three examples of how AI is used in education to improve learning outcomes.

- AI tutors provide personalized feedback and adjust lessons based on a student's progress.
- Adaptive learning platforms like Khan Academy tailor content to individual learners.
- AI tools analyze student performance data to predict areas of struggle and offer interventions.

2.

Write a haiku about the beauty of a forest during autumn.

Crimson leaves cascade,
Whispering secrets to earth—
Nature's art displayed.

3.

Generate a sample dataset in CSV (Comma-Separated Values[a]) format with 6 rows and the following columns: Name, Age, and Country.

---

a It refers to a simple, widely used text-based file format for storing tabular data, where each line represents a single data record, and the fields within that record are separated by commas.

Name,Age,Country
Alice,25,USA
Bob,30,Canada
Carlos,22,Mexico
Diana,28,UK
Eve,24,Australia
Frank,35,Germany

4.

Compare the advantages and disadvantages of solar power and wind power as renewable energy sources.

Solar power is abundant, low maintenance, and scalable, but weather-dependent and less efficient in some regions.
Wind power is efficient in windy areas and cost-effective over time but can be noisy and may harm wildlife

5.

Write a 100-word story set in a post-apocalyptic world where the protagonist discovers an ancient library.

Lena, a lone scavenger, roamed the ruins of a silent city. Ash swirled in the wind, veiling her path until she found a crumbling doorway.
Inside was an ancient library, shelves of forgotten books stretching into the shadows.
With trembling hands, she opened a tome, the words inside lighting a spark of hope.
These books held the knowledge of a lost civilization, wisdom that could rebuild the shattered world.
Lena vowed to protect them, knowing their survival might ensure humanity's.
In the quiet, the library whispered its secrets, waiting for the world to listen once more.

2.9 Conclusion

- ChatGPT can handle a variety of tasks, from simple conversations to complex problem-solving.
- Crafting effective prompts is key to getting useful responses.
- Always verify critical information provided by ChatGPT, especially for research purposes. Check the result with an expert.
- Practice refining your questions and experimenting with prompts for the best results.

By mastering the techniques outlined in this chapter, users can harness the full potential of ChatGPT. Its adaptability ensures that it can meet diverse needs, from technical problem-solving to creative exploration.

Clear questions lead to insightful answers. Refine, iterate, and innovate with ChatGPT.

Figure 2.10: ChatGPT can handle a variety of tasks....

3 Introducing AC

Let this chapter guide you in making the most of ChatGPT by simply remembering to ask.

3.1 The Unexpected Side of ChatGPT

Artificial intelligence has seamlessly integrated into our daily lives, handling tasks like delivering weather updates or managing grocery orders. Yet, *Ask ChatGPT*—let's call it **AC** (there will be no **DC**)—stands apart by transcending the mundane. It doesn't just answer questions; it collaborates with you, sparking creativity and offering solutions in ways that feel almost human. Sometimes, even better.

Ask ChatGPT encourages you to ask ChatGPT—even when doing so feels counterintuitive.

Picture this: You're stuck writing a personal statement for your dream job. The words feel flat and uninspired. Frustrated, you turn to **AC**, expecting a modest assist. Instead, **AC** guides you in crafting a compelling narrative, suggesting thoughtful phrases and fresh ideas that elevate your story. It's like having a seasoned mentor by your side, helping you shine.

Figure 3.1: Mentor.

That's the magic of **AC**. It thrives in uncertainty, uncovering surprising insights where traditional tools falter. Whether brainstorming a new business model, refining creative work, or venturing into uncharted territory, **AC** adapts and evolves, offering tailored support. It's not just about finding answers—it's about the journey of discovery.

In this chapter, we'll explore the extraordinary potential of **AC**. Beyond serving as a digital assistant, you'll see how it transforms into a creative collaborator and a brainstorming partner. Let's dive into the unexpected ways **AC** can inspire and surprise you.

https://doi.org/10.1515/9783111710808-004

3.2 Discovering Surprising Help

Most tools operate predictably—they provide results but rarely surprise. Enter **AC**, with its remarkable ability to deliver the unexpected.

Imagine you need a captivating story to kick off a presentation. Instead of offering generic suggestions, **AC** crafts a vivid, tailor-made narrative perfectly aligned with your audience's interests. It's more than just helpful—it's insightful, bringing a level of creativity and nuance that feels uniquely personal.

3.3 Nonintuitive Help

We all face situations where traditional solutions fall short—abstract challenges or moments when clear answers seem out of reach. These are the scenarios where **AC** truly excels, offering perspectives and solutions that go beyond the conventional.

3.4 Nonintuitive Scenarios

The true power of **AC** lies in asking the right questions. Tackling non-intuitive challenges requires prompts designed to inspire creativity and encourage lateral thinking. Here's how to unlock its full potential:

Set the Scene

Provide detailed context to enable **AC** to generate tailored, nuanced responses.

Example. Instead of asking, "How do I promote sustainability?" try, "Imagine you're designing a campaign to inspire urban millennials to embrace sustainability. What fun and engaging strategies might work?"

Pose Hypotheticals

Encourage **AC** to explore "what-if" scenarios for creative and insightful solutions.

Example. "What if a company introduced a four-day workweek without reducing salaries? What challenges and benefits might arise?"

Chain Your Questions

Break down complex issues into smaller, more focused prompts to build comprehensive insights.

Example. Start with, "What are common pitfalls of remote team collaboration?" Then follow up with, "How can we create a virtual environment that fosters spontaneous teamwork?"

Request Alternative Angles

Encourage **AC** to think beyond conventional approaches.

Example. "What are some counterintuitive ways to increase customer loyalty that don't rely on discounts?"

3.5 Real Stories: When AC Surprised Us

Elena's Writer's Block Breakthrough

Situation: Elena Shrick, a freelance writer, was struggling with creative stagnation while drafting her fantasy novel.

How AC Helped:

- Provided fresh ideas for character development and world-building.
- Suggested unique plot twists and alternative storylines to expand her narrative.

Outcome: With **AC**'s assistance, Elena overcame her writer's block and reinvigorated her project with renewed enthusiasm and creativity.

Figure 3.2: Elena Shrick.

Figure 3.3: James Brian.

James Brian's Remote Team Revolution

Situation: James Brian, a manager at a tech startup, struggled to foster collaboration and engagement among his remote team members.

How AC Helped:

- Proposed strategies for virtual team-building activities to enhance morale.
- Recommended tools and techniques for personalized communication and feedback.

Outcome: James successfully improved team cohesion and productivity by implementing these innovative solutions—and even managed to lose some weight in the process!

Sara's E-Commerce Evolution

Situation: Sara Schulz, an entrepreneur looking to expand her small retail business, faced significant challenges in scaling her operations.

How AC Helped:

- Conducted market research to identify and target key demographics.
- Suggested strategies for customer engagement and effective advertising campaigns.
- Recommended user-friendly enhancements for her online store to improve the customer experience.

Figure 3.4: Sara Schulz.

Outcome: By implementing targeted advertising and streamlining her e-commerce platform, Sara achieved increased sales and higher customer satisfaction.

3.6 Buying a TV on Sale

I wanted to buy a 40" TV, so I turned to Google:

> I want to buy a 40" TV, best sales price.

Google presented an overwhelming list of links: Best Buy, Amazon, Rtings.com, New York Times, Reddit, Walmart, TechRadar, Tom's Guide, EC3.us, Sam's Club, Target, Costco, eBay, PCMag, CNET, Variety, Review Maniac, LG, and many more.

Estimating the time it would take to sift through these links, compare models, and check prices? Definitely more than five minutes...(LOL).

Next, I asked ChatGPT the same question. ChatGPT advised that as of November 30, 2024, several retailers are offering significant discounts on 40-inch televisions during Black Friday sales.

Some notable deals:

TCL 40" S3 S-Class 1080p FHD LED Smart TV.

Available at Best Buy for $99.99, discounted from the original price of $229.99...

ChatGPT provided five items, each with the original price, the discounted price, and the retailer.

Time to decision: one minute.

3.7 Conclusion: Embracing the Unexpected

AC is more than just a digital assistant—it's a catalyst for creativity and a reliable problem-solving companion.

For a broader range of inspiring examples, explore Chapter 4.

Figure 3.5: Embracing the unexpected.

Part II: **ChatGPT Redux**

4 ChatGPT for Collaborative Creativity

Collaborative Creativity refers to the process of generating innovative ideas or works of art through the combined efforts of a group. By leveraging the diverse perspectives and skills of multiple contributors, this approach often produces results that are more impactful and dynamic than what a single individual could achieve.

In this chapter, ChatGPT takes on the role of a creative collaborator, enhancing and inspiring the creative process.

4.1 Creative Writing

One of ChatGPT's greatest strengths is its ability to assist with creative writing. From developing plotlines to crafting poetry, ChatGPT provides fresh perspectives and sparks of inspiration.

Figure 4.1: Creative writer.

https://doi.org/10.1515/9783111710808-006

Example 1: Story Development

A novelist working on a sci-fi epic turns to ChatGPT for ideas to build a dystopian society.

> Describe a futuristic world where water is the most valuable resource, and society is divided into those who have it and those who don't.

In the year 2147, the world is governed by the Hydro Lords, who control the Earth's last freshwater reserves. Underground rebels fight for access, leading to a clandestine trade in 'aqua gems'.

Example 2: Poetry Creation

ChatGPT aids a poet in crafting a limerick.

> Write a limerick about a mathematician who works very hard on a proof that turns out to be incorrect.

There once was a math-loving sleuth,
Who toiled on a long, tricky proof.
With a smile quite bright,
He worked through the night,
But alas, the result was uncouth!

4.2 Screenwriting and Dialogues

ChatGPT can serve as a creative collaborator on screenwriting projects, generating compelling dialogues and scene ideas.

Example 3: Scene Ideas

A filmmaker seeks inspiration for a dramatic opening to a thriller.

> Describe an opening scene for a mystery movie set in a coastal town.

The camera pans over crashing waves under a full moon. A woman in a red coat runs along the beach, clutching a letter. She pauses near an old lighthouse, only to disappear into the shadows.

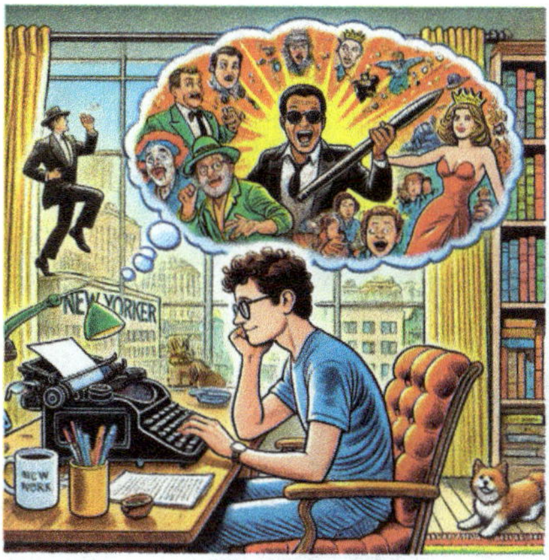

Figure 4.2: Screenwriter at work.

Example 4: Character Dialogues

ChatGPT assists in crafting a tense exchange between a detective and a robbery suspect.

Write a tense dialogue between a detective and a suspect in a robbery case.

Detective: We have your fingerprints at the scene. Care to explain? Suspect: I've already told you, I was nowhere near that store. Detective: Funny, the security footage says otherwise. Suspect: Maybe your cameras lie as much as you do.

4.3 Art and Design

Artists and designers can leverage ChatGPT to brainstorm themes, generate creative prompts, or craft descriptions for visual projects.

Example 5: Theme Suggestions for Art

An artist seeks inspiration for abstract painting themes centered on "time".

Suggest three themes for an abstract painting about 'time'.

The Fragility of Time: A swirling interplay of broken clocks and shifting sands.
Eternal Cosmos: A vibrant clash of galaxies, stars, and celestial forms.
Urban Solitude: Stark geometries and muted tones depicting cityscapes.

Figure 4.3: The fragility of time.

Example 6: Title Generation

Propose a title for a photography series on urban decay.

Whispers of Forgotten Cities.

4.4 Music and Lyric Writing

ChatGPT can assist in songwriting and music composition, acting as both a lyrical partner and an inspiration generator.

Example 7: Lyric Assistance

Write a verse for a song about overcoming challenges.

Through the storm, I found my way,
The night gave birth to brighter days,
Each step, a story I could tell,
I rose from where the shadows fell.

Example 8: Genre Fusion

Suggest a concept for blending jazz and electronic music.

A futuristic jazz lounge set in space, with synth waves blending seamlessly with smooth saxophone riffs.

4.5 Game Development

Game developers can use ChatGPT to assist with character development, world-building, and storytelling.

Example 9: Character Design

Create a backstory for a rogue character in a fantasy RPG (Role-Playing Game).

Kira Shadowthorn grew up in the slums of Eldermire, mastering the art of stealth to survive. Betrayed by her closest ally, she now seeks vengeance while navigating the shadows as a mercenary with a code: NHI (Never Harm the Innocent).

Example 10: World-Building

Describe the political structure of a magical kingdom ruled by wizards.

Figure 4.4: A rogue character in an RPG.

> The Arcane Council governs Arcadion, with each council member representing a school of magic. Beneath them, guilds manage day-to-day affairs, while an enchanted oracle serves as the kingdom's impartial judge.

4.6 Collaborative Problem-Solving

ChatGPT is a brainstorming partner for non-traditional creative challenges, such as developing innovative marketing campaigns or product designs.

Example 11: Marketing Campaigns

> Suggest a marketing campaign for an eco-friendly water bottle.

> Tagline: 'Refill Your Future'
> Campaign idea: Share photos of your water bottle in diverse locations, earning points for each refill logged in the app.

Example 12: Product Design

Describe a futuristic design for a smartwatch.

A sleek, transparent band with holographic projections for notifications. Powered by kinetic energy, it includes AI-driven wellness tracking and real-time language translation.

Figure 4.5: A magic band watch.

4.7 Ethical Considerations

While ChatGPT unlocks new creative possibilities, it also introduces important ethical challenges:

- Ensuring originality: Safeguard against plagiarism by verifying that outputs are unique and properly attributed.
- Acknowledging AI's role: Clearly credit ChatGPT's contributions in co-created works to maintain transparency.
- Preventing misuse: Avoid using ChatGPT to generate harmful, deceptive, or manipulative content.

4.8 Conclusion

ChatGPT's versatility makes it a powerful collaborator across diverse creative fields. By blending human intuition with AI-generated insights, creators can explore innovative ideas and refine their work with greater precision. As its potential for collaborative creativity continues to expand, ChatGPT is reshaping the intersection of art, problem-solving, and technology.

5 Multimodal ChatGPT

In the context of artificial intelligence, *modality* refers to a specific channel through which information is processed by an AI system. Modalities include visual, textual, auditory, and tactile inputs.

Multimodal AI integrates multiple modalities—such as text and images—into a unified system. For ChatGPT, this typically involves combining text with images.

5.1 Introduction

Artificial intelligence has traditionally been dominated by single-modality systems, focusing on processing a single type of input, such as text, images, audio, or video. However, human communication is inherently multimodal, seamlessly blending speech, gestures, visual cues, and contextual information to convey meaning.

The advent of multimodal AI systems, including the latest iterations of ChatGPT, marks a significant evolution. By integrating multiple modalities, these systems more closely mimic human communication and understanding, enabling richer interactions and deeper insights.

This chapter explores the concept of multimodal AI, delves into how ChatGPT leverages multimodal capabilities, and examines the broad implications of this innovation across various fields. Through detailed examples and use cases, we illustrate how this technology is transforming both everyday tasks and addressing complex challenges.

5.2 The Concept of Multimodal AI

Definition of Multimodal AI

Multimodal AI refers to an AI system capable of processing and responding to multiple types of input, including:
- Text: Natural language, documents, or written instructions.
- Images: Photographs, diagrams, charts, or other visual data.
- Audio: Speech, sound patterns, or other auditory signals.
- Video: Dynamic visual data, often accompanied by audio cues.

By integrating these inputs, multimodal systems can produce responses that are richer, more nuanced, and contextually relevant.

https://doi.org/10.1515/9783111710808-007

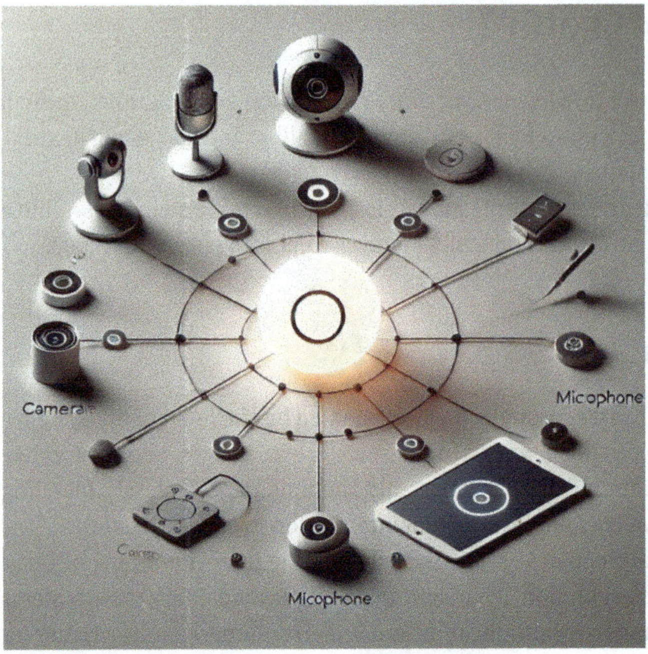

Figure 5.1: Multimodal AI.

Why Multimodal AI?

The need for multimodal AI stems from the complexity of real-world scenarios, where humans rarely rely on a single modality to interpret their surroundings. Consider these examples:

- A teacher combines diagrams with verbal explanations to clarify a concept.
- A doctor evaluates a patient's verbal description of symptoms alongside medical images, such as X-rays or MRIs.
- A driver processes traffic signs, road conditions, and auditory cues like horns to navigate safely.

To emulate human-like intelligence and perform effectively in these scenarios, AI systems must integrate and process diverse multimodal inputs.

5.3 ChatGPT as a Multimodal Assistant

Overview of Multimodal Capabilities

Recent iterations of ChatGPT have introduced multimodal capabilities, allowing it to:

- Analyze images provided by users, such as screenshots, photographs, or hand-drawn sketches.
- Respond to questions by combining insights from visual and textual inputs for enhanced comprehension.
- Assist in creative tasks by integrating text prompts with visual elements to produce cohesive results.

These advancements make ChatGPT a more versatile and effective tool for addressing a wide range of user needs.

Examples of Multimodal Interactions

Example 1 (Image Interpretation). A user uploads a picture of a math problem written on paper. ChatGPT can:

- Recognize the handwritten equations.
- Provide a step-by-step solution.
- Offer explanations tailored to the user's level of understanding.

Example 2 (Technical Troubleshooting). A user uploads a screenshot of an error message from a software application. ChatGPT can:

- Identify the error based on the image.
- Suggest possible fixes by analyzing the context.
- Provide step-by-step guidance to resolve the issue.

Example 3 (Creative Design). A user provides a text description, such as:

```
Generate a minimalist logo with a tree and a mountain
in the background.
```

ChatGPT can:

- Generate an image that aligns with the description.
- Refine the design based on user feedback, such as:
  `Make the tree larger and the mountain snow-capped.`

5.4 Applications of Multimodal AI

Education

Multimodal AI is transforming education by integrating text, images, and videos to create interactive learning experiences. Examples include:
- Explaining physics concepts with animated diagrams alongside detailed text explanations.
- Assisting language learners with pronunciation by providing audio examples and synchronized textual transcripts.
- Offering personalized tutoring with text-based quizzes and visual feedback to adapt to the learner's needs.

Healthcare

Multimodal AI enhances patient care and medical practices by:
- Analyzing medical images (e. g., X-rays, MRIs) in conjunction with patient-reported symptoms.
- Generating detailed diagnostic reports that combine textual descriptions with annotated images.
- Assisting in telemedicine by processing video consultations, recognizing visual cues, and transcribing conversations in real-time.

This topic is covered in detail in Chapter 10.

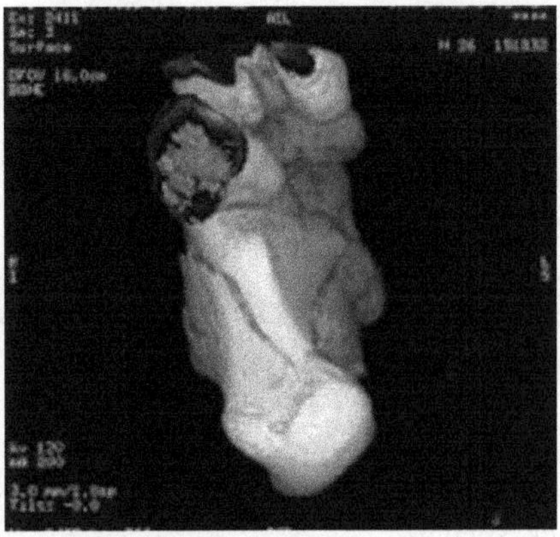

Figure 5.2: Medical image analysis.

Creative Industries

Artists, writers, and designers leverage multimodal AI to enhance creativity and efficiency. Examples include:
- Generating illustrations or concept art based on textual prompts.
- Writing stories or scripts that incorporate visual elements to enrich the narrative.
- Supporting video editing by analyzing footage and providing improvement suggestions.

Everyday Assistance

Multimodal AI supports daily tasks in innovative ways, such as:
- Designing presentations by generating slides that seamlessly integrate text and visuals.
- Interpreting scanned documents, including contracts or handwritten notes, and extracting relevant information.
- Assisting with home improvement projects by analyzing photos of spaces and offering design suggestions.

5.5 Personalized Language Learning in German

This section presents a detailed example of how ChatGPT, with its multimodal capabilities, can transform German language learning by integrating text, audio, and visual elements. The example highlights the benefits of such an application.

Scenario: Learning German with ChatGPT

Imagine Emily, a college student learning German, who aims to improve her vocabulary, pronunciation, and contextual understanding. ChatGPT provides her with an interactive and personalized learning experience using multimodal inputs and outputs.

Step 1: Vocabulary Expansion

Emily begins by asking, “Teach me some useful German phrases for traveling.” ChatGPT responds with a list of phrases and their translations:

- Wo ist die Toilette?" – Where is the bathroom?"
- Wie viel kostet das?" – How much does this cost?"
- Ich brauche Hilfe." – "I need help."

To enhance understanding, ChatGPT also displays images illustrating the context of each phrase:
- A restroom sign for "Wo ist die Toilette?"
- A bustling market scene for "Wie viel kostet das?"

Figure 5.3: Bathroom signs in Germany.

Step 2: Pronunciation Practice

ChatGPT includes an audio component, allowing Emily to hear each phrase spoken by a native German speaker. She records her pronunciation using her device's microphone, and ChatGPT evaluates her input, providing detailed feedback such as:
- "Your pronunciation of 'Toilette' is slightly off. Focus on the final 'e' sound."

Step 3: Contextual Roleplay

To reinforce her learning, ChatGPT creates a roleplay scenario using text, audio, and images. In this example, ChatGPT acts as a shopkeeper in a German market:

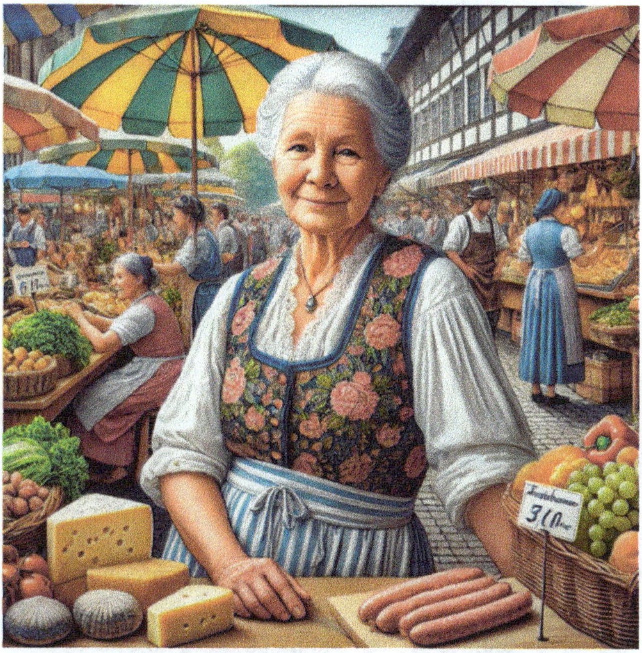

Figure 5.4: Wie kann ich Ihnen helfen?

> **ChatGPT:** Guten Tag! Willkommen in meinem Laden. Wie kann ich Ihnen helfen?"
> **Emily:** Wie viel kostet das?"
> **ChatGPT:** "Das kostet zehn Euro. Möchten Sie es kaufen?"

As Emily interacts, ChatGPT dynamically adapts its responses and displays relevant images, such as the item being discussed.

Step 4: Visual Grammar Tutorials

To teach grammar, ChatGPT utilizes diagrams and visual aids. For instance, when explaining verb conjugations, it provides a clear and concise chart:

Subjekt	Verb (Sprechen)	Übersetzung
Ich	spreche	I speak
Du	sprichst	You speak
Er/Sie/Es	spricht	He/She/It speaks

Step 5: Progress Tracking

ChatGPT tracks Emily's progress across sessions by generating a personalized dashboard that summarizes:

- Vocabulary mastered.
- Pronunciation accuracy (e. g., 85 % correct).
- Grammar topics covered.

Based on her performance, ChatGPT suggests new topics or areas of focus, ensuring Emily's learning journey remains tailored to her individual needs.

5.6 Challenges in Multimodal AI

Technical Challenges

- Data Fusion: Integrating data from different modalities while preserving contextual meaning and coherence.
- Scalability: Managing large volumes of multimodal data in real-time applications without compromising performance.
- Model Complexity: Designing architectures capable of understanding and leveraging relationships across multiple modalities effectively.

Ethical Challenges

- Bias: Ensuring fairness across modalities, as biases in training data can lead to inequitable outputs.
- Privacy: Safeguarding user data, particularly when handling sensitive content like images or audio.
- Misuse: Preventing the misuse of multimodal AI for harmful purposes, such as generating deepfakes or misleading content.

5.7 Implications for the Future

Transformative Potential

The integration of multimodal capabilities into systems like ChatGPT has far-reaching implications:

- In Accessibility: Supporting visually or hearing-impaired individuals by converting text to audio, images to text, and vice versa.
- In Research: Assisting scientists by processing and correlating data from diverse sources, such as textual reports and visual datasets.
- In Communication: Enhancing virtual collaboration tools by seamlessly integrating text, images, and video for richer interactions.

5.8 Conclusion

Multimodal AI represents a significant leap forward in artificial intelligence. By enabling systems like ChatGPT to process and integrate diverse inputs, it unlocks transformative possibilities across education, healthcare, creativity, and beyond. As this technology continues to evolve, addressing technical and ethical challenges will be crucial to realizing its full potential responsibly.

Part III: **Stories About Small Companies**

6 MonteCalc

This is the story of how I failed to become a millionaire.

6.1 Two Valuable Numerical Methods

I was fortunate to have my Probability Course taught by Alfréd Rényi, a renowned researcher in the Monte Carlo Method. For those less fortunate, here's a brief introduction to both the Monte Carlo Method and Matrix Decompositions. Feel free to skip this section.

The Monte Carlo Method is a statistical technique that uses random sampling to solve problems that are deterministic in principle. It is widely applied in numerical integration, optimization, and fields such as finance, engineering, physics, quantum mechanics, and operations research.

Matrix Decompositions involve breaking matrices into products of simpler matrices, simplifying complex linear algebra problems. These decompositions are es-

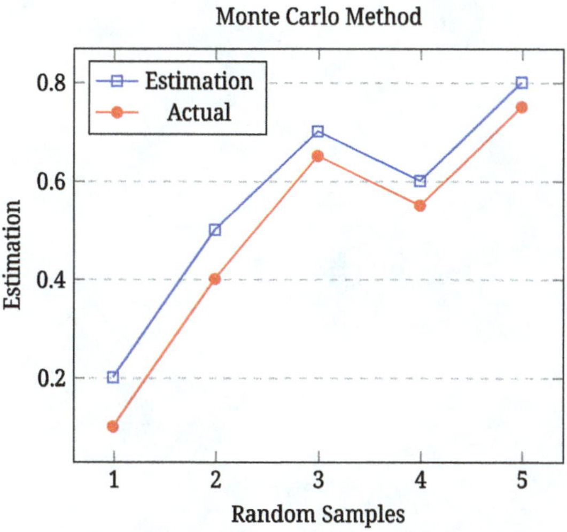

Figure 6.1: Monte Carlo Method: estimation vs. actual.

https://doi.org/10.1515/9783111710808-009

sential in numerical applications, enhancing computational efficiency and stability in areas like engineering, computer science, and data science.

With these foundational concepts explained, let's dive into the founding story of MonteCalc.

6.2 Founding Story

Professor Friedrich (Fred) Szabo,[1] a prominent researcher in the Monte Carlo Method, had a breakthrough one evening while tackling a challenging simulation problem. During a coffee break, he envisioned combining the Monte Carlo Method with Matrix Decompositions. Seeking expertise in the latter, he contacted his colleague, Professor Andrew (Nyul) Azstalos. Over a nostalgic dinner, as they reminisced about their days as graduate students, the idea for MonteCalc was born.

In 2023, Fred and Nyul founded MonteCalc (not to be confused with the Montessori Calculator), aiming to develop cutting-edge applications for various industries.

> "It started as a late-night idea over coffee and evolved into a company pushing the boundaries of computational simulations," recalls Fred Szabo.

Figure 6.2: Montessori calculator.

1 Names have been changed to protect the rich.

Starting a company from scratch was no small feat, but Fred and Nyul's complementary expertise and vision propelled MonteCalc forward. They assembled a team of eight programmers, a secretary, and a part-time technical writer.

6.3 Products and Services

MonteCalc quickly became a leader in advanced simulation tools by integrating the Monte Carlo Method with Matrix Decompositions.

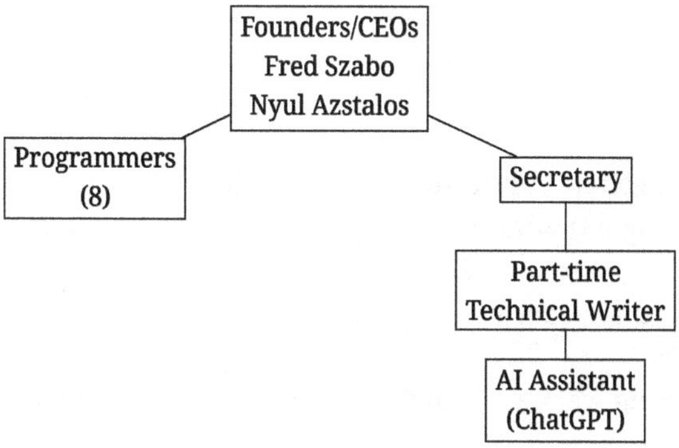

Figure 6.3: Organizational structure of MonteCalc.

MonteCalc Suite

The flagship MonteCalc Suite offers several specialized modules:

- **MonteCalc Finance:** Tools for risk assessment and financial forecasting. For instance, it helped a major investment firm optimize their portfolio diversification, resulting in a 15 % increase in predicted returns.
- **MonteCalc Engineering:** Solutions for reliability engineering and process optimization. MonteCalc Engineering was used to simulate stress tests for a new skyscraper, reducing costs by 20 %.
- **MonteCalc Data Science:** Advanced tools for big data analysis, machine learning, and predictive analytics. A tech startup employed MonteCalc Data Science to speed up their AI model training, cutting processing time in half.

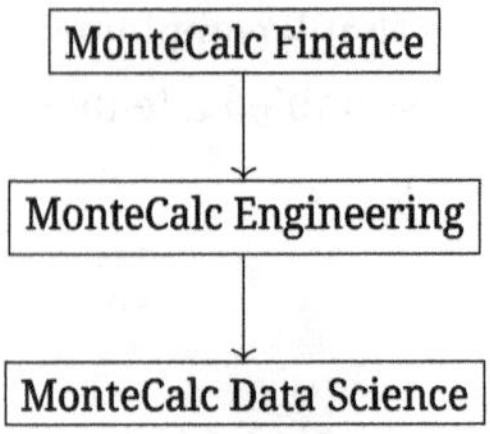

Figure 6.4: MonteCalc Suite modules.

Simulations and Consulting

MonteCalc also provides custom simulations tailored to unique client needs. This service is ideal for organizations with specialized requirements beyond the scope of off-the-shelf software.

To support clients, MonteCalc offers consulting services, including:
- *Strategy Development:* Helping organizations integrate simulation techniques into operations.
- *Technical Support:* Providing ongoing technical assistance to maximize the value of MonteCalc's products.
- *Training Programs:* Conducting workshops and training sessions on the effective use of MonteCalc's software.

> "MonteCalc not only solved our immediate challenges but helped us reshape our entire simulation workflow," said a client in the automotive industry.

6.4 Future Plans

MonteCalc's forward-thinking approach and commitment to innovation have positioned it for continued growth. Key areas of future development include:

Product Development

- Developing industry-specific modules for healthcare, energy, and environmental science.
- Enhancing AI-driven simulations for greater accuracy and efficiency.
- Expanding into mobile and cloud-based solutions.

Geographic Expansion

- Establishing partnerships in Europe, Asia, and South America.
- Collaborating with international academic institutions for research.

Social Impact

MonteCalc is committed to addressing global challenges by using its technology for climate modeling and renewable energy optimization, reflecting a vision of sustainability and responsibility.

7 Kimo Sabe Mezcal

Mezcal: An agave plant
Mezcal: An alcoholic drink made from the sap of an agave

Figure 7.1: The location of Kimo Sabe Mezcal, an agave plant, and a bottle of mezcal.

7.1 Introduction

Kimo Sabe Mezcal is a standout player in the artisanal spirits market.[1] With a mission to craft mezcal that honors tradition while embracing innovation, Kimo Sabe Mezcal has evolved from a local favorite to a brand with national and international appeal. This growth stems from its commitment to quality and the strategic use of technology, such as ChatGPT, to improve operations and enhance customer engagement.

In this chapter, we explore the company's journey, its business model, and how the integration of AI has impacted its operations.

7.2 Company Background

Founded by father-daughter duo Jim and Ashley Walsh, Kimo Sabe Mezcal was born out of a passion for creating a high-quality mezcal that blends traditional Mexican craftsmanship with modern production techniques. Their mission was to bring the rich cultural heritage of mezcal to a wider audience while preserving its authenticity.

The journey began in Oaxaca, Mexico, where the founders collaborated with local mezcaleros. By leveraging generations of expertise and traditional methods,

1 Artisanal spirits differ from industrially produced ones in that they rely heavily on human expertise throughout the production process, from fermentation and distillation to aging and bottling. This hands-on approach ensures unique, high-quality flavors.

https://doi.org/10.1515/9783111710808-010

Figure 7.2: Jim and Ashley Walsh.

they created a product that stands apart from competitors often reliant on mass production.

Business Model and Operations

Kimo Sabe Mezcal operates with an artisanal production model centered around sustainability and quality. The agave is sourced from sustainable farms in Oaxaca and harvested at peak maturity to maximize flavor. Traditional methods such as slow roasting in earthen pits, natural fermentation, and copper distillation are complemented by modern quality control measures.

The company offers three primary varieties of mezcal:

- **Joven:** Smooth and approachable.
- **Reposado:** Complex and aged.
- **Añejo:** Rich and matured.

Additionally, Kimo Sabe Mezcal has introduced innovative infused varieties and limited editions to keep the brand fresh and appealing. Products are sold primarily through the company's website, ensuring a direct-to-consumer model that maintains control over the customer experience. The brand also has a presence in select retail stores and bars.

Cultural Heritage of Mezcal

Mezcal is more than a beverage—it is a cultural symbol deeply rooted in Mexican history and traditions. For centuries, mezcal has been crafted using time-honored techniques passed down through generations. It plays a significant role in celebrations and rituals, embodying the spirit of community and heritage. Kimo Sabe Mezcal honors this legacy by blending traditional methods with modern innovation, ensuring the essence of mezcal remains intact.

Sustainability Initiatives

Kimo Sabe Mezcal is committed to sustainability, sourcing agave from eco-friendly farms and ensuring responsible harvesting practices. By using renewable energy in their production facilities and minimizing waste, the company actively reduces its environmental footprint. Their long-term vision includes reforestation projects and collaborations with local communities to promote sustainable agriculture.

Organizational Structure

Kimo Sabe Mezcal operates with a lean and efficient team, typically fewer than 50 employees, organized into key departments:

- **Executive Leadership:** Led by founders Jim and Ashley Walsh, ensuring alignment with the company's vision and values.
- **Production:** Based in Oaxaca, this team handles every stage of the mezcal-making process.
- **Marketing and Sales:** Responsible for promotions, online presence, and distributor relationships.

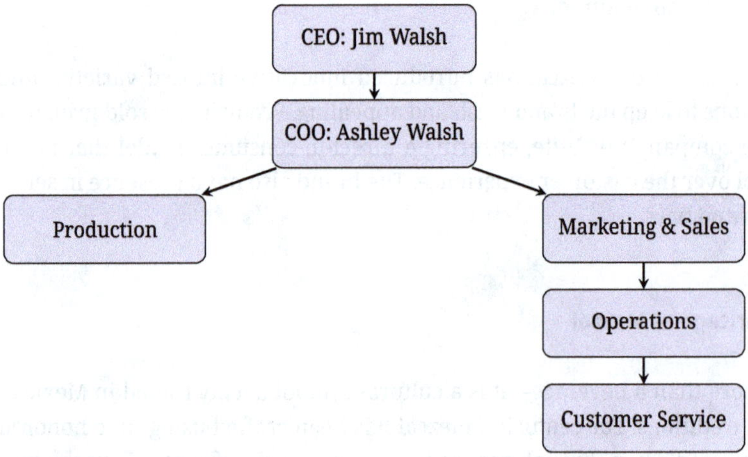

Figure 7.3: Organizational chart of Kimo Sabe Mezcal.

- **Customer Service:** Ensures positive experiences for customers through prompt support.
- **Operations:** Manages inventory, logistics, and financial oversight.

7.3 Implementation of ChatGPT

Case Study: ChatGPT's First Month

During the initial month of deployment, ChatGPT was tasked with managing an unexpected surge in customer inquiries following the launch of a new limited-edition mezcal. By providing instant and accurate responses, the AI handled 85 % of inquiries autonomously, freeing up human staff to focus on complex issues. This seamless handling of high demand resulted in a 15 % boost in customer satisfaction ratings and ensured the successful promotion of the new product.

Continuous Learning and Feedback

Regular feedback loops are integral to ChatGPT's success at Kimo Sabe Mezcal. Customer feedback, combined with performance analytics, is used to refine the AI's responses and expand its knowledge base. For instance, customer queries about mezcal pairing inspired the development of a recipe suggestion feature, adding value to the overall experience.

7.4 Future Prospects

Future Opportunities with AI

As AI technology evolves, Kimo Sabe Mezcal plans to explore virtual mezcal-tasting experiences. This feature would use AI to simulate taste profiles, allowing customers to discover their preferences online. Additionally, AI-driven supply chain optimization could enhance efficiency, reducing costs and further supporting the company's sustainability goals.

8 WoodCraft

Decades ago, I imported a few pieces of furniture from Denmark. When it arrived, I was amazed. I expected it to be nice, but I did not anticipate that the hidden parts would be as meticulously finished as the visible ones.

This tradition of excellence is upheld by Toronto's WoodCraft.

Figure 8.1: Toronto's WoodCraft.

8.1 The Challenge

Overview WoodCraft is a renowned custom furniture maker celebrated for its craftsmanship and personalized designs. Founded in 2005, the company has built a reputation for creating high-quality furniture tailored to customers' unique needs. Its commitment to sustainability and use of locally sourced materials distinguish it in a competitive market.

The Problem WoodCraft faced challenges in managing a growing volume of customer inquiries, which required detailed responses about products, customization options, and order statuses. The traditional customer service model was inefficient, leading to backlogs and lost sales opportunities.

Impact The inefficiency in handling inquiries caused customer dissatisfaction and trust issues, impacting revenue. The customer service team experienced burnout and emphasizing the need for an efficient solution.

https://doi.org/10.1515/9783111710808-011

Analysis of the Problem

Customer Service Team The customer service team struggled with the volume and complexity of inquiries across multiple channels, including email, phone, and social media. Their capacity was overstretched, causing delays.

Customer Inquiries Inquiries ranged from product availability questions to custom design requests. The complexity and volume required detailed and personalized responses, increasing the workload significantly.

Delayed Responses Slow responses frustrated customers, leading some to turn to competitors. This eroded trust and damaged the company's reputation.

Figure 8.2: Dining room.

Figure 8.3: Living room.

Potential Solutions

Initial Strategies WoodCraft considered hiring more staff and using traditional customer service tools. However, these options were costly and did not address the root issues of scalability and efficiency.

Innovative Solutions The company explored AI solutions like ChatGPT for handling high volumes of inquiries. AI promised scalability, efficiency, and the ability to provide personalized responses, relieving the human team of repetitive tasks.

8.2 Implementing ChatGPT

Selecting ChatGPT ChatGPT was chosen for its advanced capabilities, cost-effectiveness, and potential for continuous learning. A thorough analysis of AI options confirmed its suitability for WoodCraft's needs.

Integration Process Integration involved defining ChatGPT's responsibilities, training it on product and service details, and testing its performance during a pilot phase. Successful testing led to full integration across all customer interaction channels.

Training ChatGPT ChatGPT was trained with detailed knowledge of WoodCraft's products, customization options, pricing, and brand values. It was also equipped with customer sentiment analysis to ensure an empathetic response style. Regular updates ensured the AI remained accurate and effective.

Challenges in Training Training ChatGPT required addressing edge cases, such as unusual customization requests or ambiguous inquiries. These scenarios were carefully programmed and tested to ensure the AI's reliability.

See also Chapter 9.

Enhanced Scalability and Sustainability

Scalability ChatGPT was designed to scale with the business. As WoodCraft's customer base grows, the AI can handle increasing inquiry volumes without requiring additional staffing.

Environmental Impact The implementation of AI has reduced paper-based communication and optimized workflows, contributing to WoodCraft's sustainability goals. By streamlining operations, the company minimizes waste and supports its commitment to environmental responsibility.

Functionality of ChatGPT

Customer Interactions ChatGPT efficiently handles initial interactions, providing instant responses to product inquiries, customization requests, and order updates. This improves customer experience and reduces wait times.

Inquiry Management The AI manages multiple inquiries simultaneously, offering detailed information and reducing the workload on the customer service team.

Virtual Assistance ChatGPT assists customers with customization choices, offering suggestions based on preferences and past orders. It enhances the process with visual aids like images and videos.

Outcome and Benefits

Improvements Response times improved from several hours to seconds, boosting customer satisfaction and loyalty. The company experienced a 30 % increase in online conversions and a 15 % rise in repeat orders.

Efficiency Gains The AI reduced the team's workload by 40 %, allowing staff to focus on complex inquiries and personalized service.

Visualization of Metrics The graph of Metrics highlights key metrics before and after ChatGPT's implementation, showing significant improvements in efficiency and satisfaction.

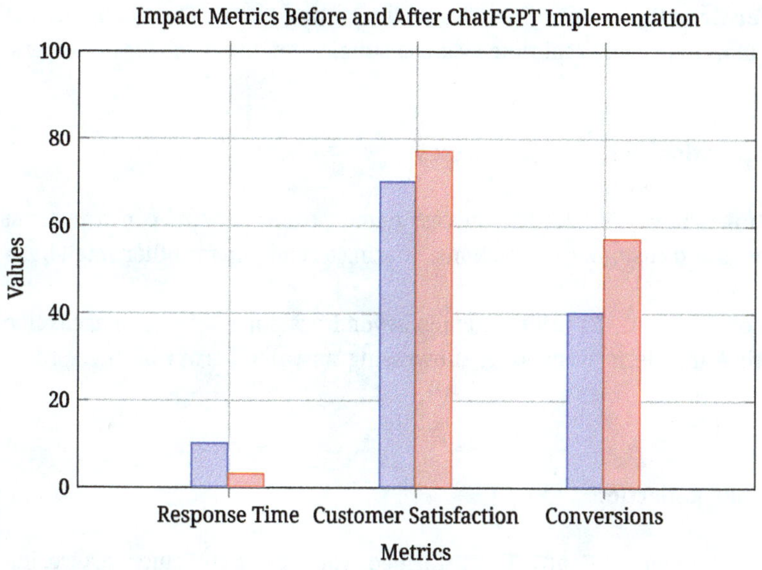

Figure 8.4: Impact metrics: Response time, customer satisfaction, and conversions.

8.3 Case Study: Customer Experiences

Examples ChatGPT guided a customer in customizing a dining table by suggesting wood types, finishes, and dimensions, leading to a smooth purchase experience.

Testimonials Customers praised the quick and accurate responses. One customer noted, "ChatGPT made the decision-making process much smoother."

Impact on Business Operations

Refocus The customer service team now focuses on high-value tasks, enhancing support for custom projects and issue resolution.

Improvements Special requests and complex customizations are handled more effectively, boosting customer trust and satisfaction.

8.4 Lessons Learned and Future Steps

Key Takeaways Effective AI integration requires thorough training and continuous updates. A balanced approach to AI and human effort is essential for success.

Future Plans WoodCraft plans to enhance ChatGPT's capabilities and explore its application in inventory management and analytics.

Potential for Growth WoodCraft envisions integrating ChatGPT with augmented reality tools to provide real-time visual customization previews for customers.

Broader Implications for Small Businesses

Learnings for Others WoodCraft's success demonstrates how AI can transform operations and customer interactions, offering a roadmap for other small businesses.

Versatility of AI ChatGPT's utility extends beyond customer service to areas like marketing and decision-making, showcasing its value across business functions.

Conclusion and Reflection

Summary Implementing ChatGPT transformed WoodCraft's customer service, improving efficiency, satisfaction, and revenue.

Reflection The experience underscores the transformative power of AI in business operations and customer service.

Final Thoughts As AI continues to evolve, WoodCraft's success serves as a model for leveraging technology to achieve growth and innovation.

Figure 8.5: Downton four door buffet & hutch.

Part IV: **ChatGPT in Industry**

9 Customer Support

In the digital age, customer support has become a cornerstone of business success. With consumers expecting rapid and accurate responses, companies are increasingly turning to artificial intelligence to meet these demands.

This is the story of how it is done.

9.1 Introduction

One of the most promising advancements in this field is ChatGPT, an advanced language model developed by OpenAI. We have seen in the earlier chapters, how this AI-driven tool has the potential to transform customer service by providing timely and precise assistance, handling routine inquiries, and enabling human agents to focus on more complex issues.

In this chapter, we will explore the intricacies of ChatGPT's training process and examine case studies that showcase its practical applications in revolutionizing customer support.

By understanding how ChatGPT is trained and implemented, we can appreciate the transformative impact it has on businesses across various industries. From e-commerce platforms to software companies and financial institutions, ChatGPT is proving to be an invaluable asset in enhancing customer satisfaction and operational efficiency.

Join us me as I delve into the world of ChatGPT, uncovering the methodologies behind its training and the real-world benefits it brings to customer support systems.

9.2 The Training Process

To appreciate how ChatGPT enhances customer support, it's essential to understand the robust training process that equips it with the ability to deliver accurate and contextually relevant responses. ChatGPT is built on the GPT-4 architecture, leveraging a combination of supervised learning, reinforcement learning, and specialized training techniques.

https://doi.org/10.1515/9783111710808-013

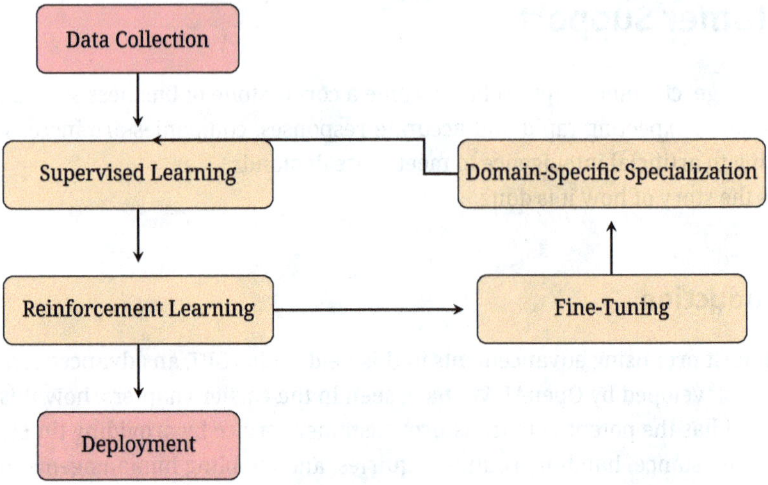

Figure 9.1: The training process.

Data Collection

The journey begins with data collection. ChatGPT is trained on a vast corpus of text data sourced from diverse origins such as books, websites, and forums. This extensive dataset helps the model learn the intricacies of human language, including grammar, context, idioms, and nuances.

Supervised Learning and Reinforcement Learning

ChatGPT is refined through a combination of supervised learning and reinforcement learning from human feedback. These processes ensure the AI generates responses that are both relevant and aligned with user expectations.

Specialization for Customer Support

To tailor ChatGPT specifically for customer support, the model undergoes additional training on specialized datasets. This includes detailed information about a company's products, services, policies, and procedures.

Continuous Learning and Adaptation

The training process doesn't end once ChatGPT is deployed. Businesses should update the model's training data to ensure it evolves to meet changing customer needs and expectations.

9.3 Future Trends

As AI technology evolves, the future of customer support is expected to include:
- **Sentiment Analysis Integration:** AI will increasingly analyze customer emotions during interactions, enabling businesses to offer empathetic and personalized responses in real-time.
- **Multimodal Support:** ChatGPT-like models will integrate voice, video, and text for a seamless omnichannel customer experience.
- **Predictive Assistance:** By analyzing historical customer data, AI can predict issues before they arise and proactively offer solutions, minimizing customer effort.
- **Advanced Personalization:** AI will use deeper customer insights to offer hyper-personalized experiences, such as tailored product recommendations or bespoke solutions.
- **AI-Human Collaboration:** Advanced tools will enable AI to assist human agents by suggesting responses, offering contextual insights, and automating follow-ups.

These advancements will continue to reshape customer support, creating more engaging and efficient interactions for businesses and customers alike.

9.4 Challenges and Ethical Considerations

While ChatGPT has transformed customer support, businesses must navigate several challenges and ethical concerns:
- **Bias in Responses:** AI models can inadvertently reflect biases present in their training data, leading to unfair or inappropriate responses. Continuous monitoring and refinement are necessary to address this issue.

- **Privacy and Data Security:** Handling sensitive customer information requires robust security measures and compliance with regulations like GDPR[1] or CCPA[2] to build trust and avoid legal risks.
- **Transparency:** Customers may not always be aware they are interacting with AI. Clear communication about the use of AI in customer support fosters trust and avoids misunderstandings.
- **Overreliance on Automation:** While AI can handle routine tasks effectively, over-automation may result in a lack of human touch, potentially frustrating customers in complex or emotionally charged situations.
- **Job Displacement:** The shift toward AI-driven customer support raises concerns about job displacement. Companies must invest in reskilling programs to support employees transitioning to new roles.

By addressing these challenges, businesses can ensure the responsible and effective implementation of AI in customer support.

9.5 Customer Feedback on AI-Driven Support

The adoption of AI-powered tools like ChatGPT has garnered diverse reactions from customers:
- **Positive Feedback:** Customers frequently praise AI-driven support for its speed, availability, and accuracy. Many appreciate the convenience of resolving issues without waiting for human agents.
- **Constructive Criticism:** Some customers note challenges such as AI's inability to handle unique or complex queries effectively, highlighting the need for seamless escalation to human agents.
- **Impact on Satisfaction Scores:** Surveys indicate that AI integration has boosted NPS (Net Promoter Scores) and CSAT (Customer Satisfaction) metrics for businesses using ChatGPT.

Analyzing customer feedback enables businesses to refine their AI strategies, ensuring a balance between automation and human intervention.

1 GDPR stands for the General Data Protection Regulation, which is a legal framework established by the European Union (EU) to regulate the collection, storage, processing, and transfer of personal data of individuals within the EU.

2 The CCPA grants California residents the following rights about personal information: Right to Know, Right to Delete, Right to Opt-Out.

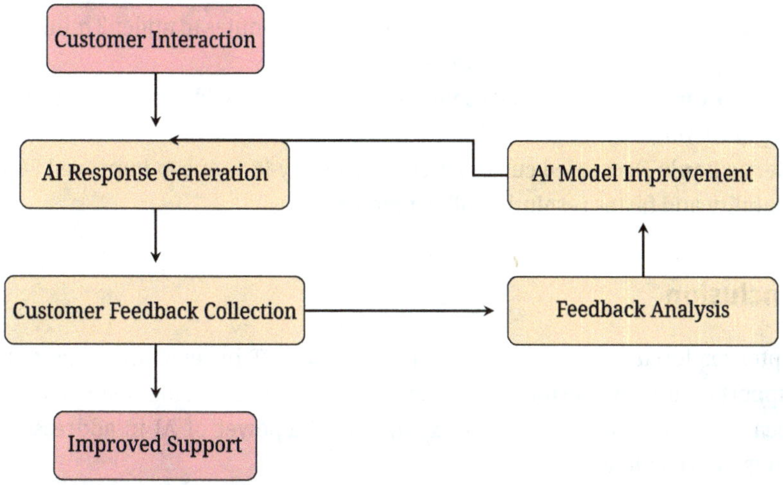

Figure 9.2: Customer feedback.

9.6 AI and Accessibility in Customer Support

ChatGPT and similar AI tools are improving accessibility for customers with diverse needs:

- **Language Support:** AI can provide real-time translations, enabling businesses to support customers across multiple languages seamlessly.
- **Inclusive Interactions:** AI models can be tailored to accommodate customers with disabilities, such as offering voice-to-text or screen reader-compatible interfaces.
- **24/7 Availability:** AI ensures that customers in different time zones or with unconventional schedules can access support whenever needed.
- **Simplified Communication:** By breaking down complex topics into simpler language, AI makes support more approachable for all users.

These capabilities allow businesses to deliver inclusive, accessible customer experiences that cater to a global audience.

9.7 Case Studies: Quantifiable Results

The integration of ChatGPT led to measurable improvements for the featured companies:

- **ShopEase:** Reduced average response time from 10 minutes to under 2 minutes, increasing customer satisfaction scores by 25 %.
- **TechSolutions:** Improved first-resolution rates by 40 %, reducing ticket backlog during peak times by 50 %.
- **FinServe Bank:** Decreased customer churn rates by 18 % due to improved 24/7 availability and faster resolution of common queries.

9.8 Conclusion

This chapter explored the transformative role of ChatGPT in revolutionizing customer support across diverse industries. From its robust training methodologies to its practical implementation, ChatGPT exemplifies the power of AI in addressing modern business challenges.

Key takeaways include:

- **Streamlined Operations:** ChatGPT automates routine tasks, freeing up human agents for complex problem-solving.
- **Enhanced Customer Satisfaction:** With prompt, accurate responses, businesses can meet customer expectations effectively.

Figure 9.3: Enhanced customer satisfaction.

- **Cost Efficiency:** By reducing the dependency on extensive human resources, ChatGPT optimizes costs while maintaining high-quality support.
- **Adaptability:** Domain-specific training ensures ChatGPT is tailored to the unique needs of industries like e-commerce, software, and banking.

As businesses continue to embrace AI, ChatGPT's ability to learn, adapt, and evolve will remain integral to providing exceptional customer experiences. Its implementation not only enhances operational efficiency but also ensures that businesses stay competitive in a rapidly evolving digital landscape.

By investing in AI-driven customer support, companies can achieve a balance of efficiency, innovation, and customer satisfaction, paving the way for future success.

10 AI in Healthcare

Artificial Intelligence (AI) is revolutionizing healthcare by introducing unparalleled efficiency and accessibility to medical practices. Through enhanced diagnostic precision and personalized treatment plans, AI is reshaping how we understand and deliver healthcare. This chapter explores the innovative ways AI is integrated into various facets of medicine, driving improved patient outcomes while addressing critical ethical and operational challenges. However, the healthcare industry, being vast and often resistant to change, poses significant hurdles to widespread adoption of AI technologies in a timely fashion.

10.1 Revolutionizing Diagnostics

AI-powered diagnostics are transforming healthcare by enabling faster and more precise disease detection. By leveraging machine learning and neural networks, AI systems analyze complex medical data, offering unprecedented accuracy and efficiency.

AI in Radiology

Radiology is among the most successful fields for AI applications. AI models can detect abnormalities in medical images such as X-rays, CT scans, and MRIs, often surpassing human performance. Examples include:

– **Lung Disease Detection:** AI models have achieved over 90 % diagnostic accuracy for detecting pneumonia and tuberculosis on chest X-rays. For instance,

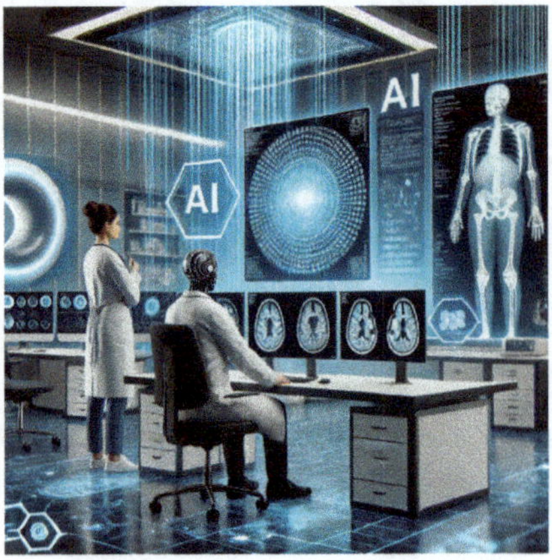

Figure 10.1: AI in radiology.

https://doi.org/10.1515/9783111710808-014

Google's DeepMind reported an 88 % sensitivity rate for identifying early-stage lung cancer.
- **Breast Cancer Screening:** A large-scale study involving over 58,000 women found that AI-assisted mammography detected more breast cancers (0.82 % vs. 0.70 %) and reduced false-positive rates (1.63 % vs. 2.39 %) compared to traditional methods.
- **Stroke Detection:** AI platforms like Viz.ai have demonstrated a reduction in treatment time by up to 90 minutes for stroke patients by automating the detection process and alerting specialists in real-time.

Predictive Diagnostics

AI excels in predictive diagnostics, analyzing patient data to proactively identify health risks:
- **Cardiovascular Health Monitoring:** AI algorithms predict atrial fibrillation with 97 % accuracy using data from wearable devices such as smartwatches.
- **Diabetes Risk Assessment:** AI-based risk prediction models, like those developed by IBM Watson Health, achieve an 89 % precision rate in identifying individuals at high risk for type 2 diabetes.
- **Cancer Risk Prediction:** AI tools that integrate genomic data achieve up to 93 % accuracy in predicting hereditary cancer risks, providing actionable insights for preventive care.

AI in Pathology

Pathology is another area where AI significantly improves diagnostic accuracy and speed:
- **Histopathological Analysis:** AI tools identify cancer markers in tissue samples with up to 96 % sensitivity, reducing diagnostic time by 70 % compared to traditional methods.
- **Quantitative Analysis:** AI systems, such as PathAI, provide precise measurements of tumor size and cellular abnormalities, aiding oncologists in developing tailored treatment plans.

Case Studies

Real-world implementations illustrate the transformative impact of AI diagnostics:

- **COVID-19 Detection:** During the pandemic, AI systems analyzed chest X-rays and CT scans with 92 % accuracy, significantly reducing the diagnostic workload in overwhelmed hospitals.
- **AI in Ophthalmology:** Google's ARDA system for diabetic retinopathy screening achieved a sensitivity rate of 89 % and a specificity rate of 91 %, making it a reliable tool for early diagnosis.
- **Skin Cancer Screening:** AI-powered smartphone apps, such as SkinVision, report an 85 % accuracy rate in identifying malignant skin lesions, providing an accessible tool for early intervention.

10.2 Patient Interaction and Virtual Assistants

AI-powered virtual assistants are transforming patient interaction by delivering immediate and personalized healthcare support. These systems bridge the gap between patients and healthcare providers, offering services ranging from appointment scheduling to symptom analysis and chronic disease management.

AI Chatbots for Healthcare Support

AI chatbots, such as Babylon Health and Ada, assist patients with a range of tasks, including:
- **Symptom Analysis:** Chatbots utilize natural language processing to interpret patients' symptom descriptions and suggest potential diagnoses. For example, Babylon Health reports a 93 % accuracy rate in matching patient-reported symptoms to likely conditions.
- **Appointment Scheduling:** Tools like Olive AI streamline administrative tasks by managing appointment bookings, reducing no-show rates by up to 15 %.
- **Medication Reminders:** Chatbots send personalized medication reminders to patients, improving adherence rates. A pilot study by MediBot demonstrated a 22 % increase in medication compliance among elderly users.

Remote Patient Monitoring

Remote patient monitoring systems powered by AI enable real-time data collection and analysis, enhancing care for patients with chronic conditions. Key applications include:

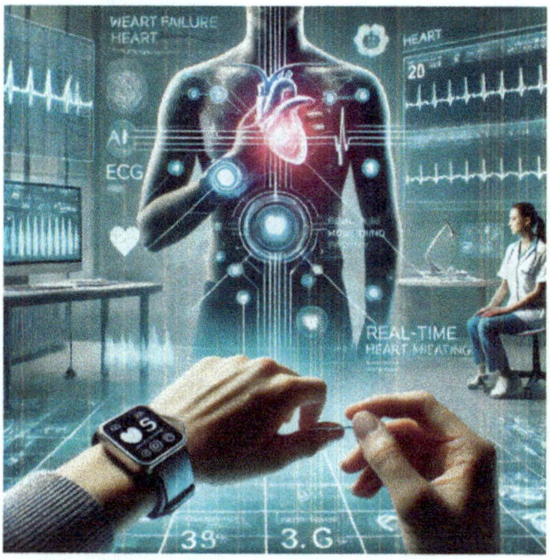

Figure 10.2: AI in heart monitoring.

- **Chronic Disease Management:** AI systems like Livongo monitor glucose levels in diabetes patients and provide actionable insights, resulting in a 29 % reduction in hypoglycemic events.
- **Heart Failure Monitoring:** Wearable devices integrated with AI platforms track cardiovascular metrics. For instance, Biofourmis has achieved a 27 % reduction in hospital readmissions for heart failure patients by detecting early warning signs.
- **Mental Health Support:** Virtual assistants like Woebot offer 24/7 mental health support, employing cognitive-behavioral therapy techniques. Studies on Woebot users show a 32 % reduction in depression and anxiety symptoms after six weeks of interaction.

Real-World Applications and Success Stories

AI-powered virtual assistants have demonstrated significant value across various healthcare settings:

- **Telemedicine Integration:** Virtual assistants are integral to telemedicine platforms, ensuring seamless patient-doctor communication. For example, Teladoc Health employs AI to pre-screen patients, saving physicians up to 15 minutes per consultation.
- **Elderly Care:** ElliQ, a robot companion for older adults, provides daily check-ins, medication reminders, and social interaction, enhancing users' quality of life. Pilot studies report a 34 % reduction in loneliness levels among ElliQ users.

- **Pandemic Support:** During the COVID-19 pandemic, AI chatbots delivered critical information about testing locations, symptoms, and vaccination schedules. The World Health Organization (WHO) chatbot supported over 13 million users globally in multiple languages.

10.3 Medical Education with ChatGPT

AI technologies, particularly ChatGPT, are revolutionizing medical education by delivering personalized and interactive learning experiences. Medical students, educators, and practitioners benefit from its ability to simplify complex topics, simulate real-world scenarios, and provide immediate feedback.

Simplifying Complex Concepts

ChatGPT excels at breaking down intricate medical concepts into accessible explanations. Examples include:

- **Human Anatomy:** ChatGPT provides step-by-step descriptions of anatomical structures and their functions, customized to the user's level of understanding.
- **Pharmacology Basics:** It explains drug mechanisms, side effects, and interactions in a conversational format, making challenging topics more approachable.
- **Clinical Pathways:** Students can review case-based clinical pathways with ChatGPT, enhancing their diagnostic reasoning and clinical decision-making skills.

Interactive Problem-Solving

Medical education increasingly emphasizes active learning, and ChatGPT supports this approach by facilitating interactive problem-solving. Applications include:

- **Clinical Case Studies:** ChatGPT generates realistic clinical scenarios, prompting students to make diagnoses and recommend treatments, fostering critical thinking.
- **Exam Preparation:** Students can practice mock questions, including multiple-choice or open-ended clinical vignettes, with ChatGPT offering instant feedback and detailed rationales.

- **Research Guidance:** ChatGPT assists students in formulating research questions, outlining study designs, and locating relevant literature, streamlining the research process.

Supporting Continuing Medical Education

For healthcare professionals, continuing education is essential, and ChatGPT enhances this process by offering:

- **On-Demand Learning:** Practitioners can stay updated on the latest medical guidelines and evidence-based practices using ChatGPT during clinical downtime.
- **Specialized Training:** ChatGPT provides in-depth insights into niche fields, such as pediatric cardiology or neuro-oncology, helping professionals expand their expertise.
- **Skill Refresher:** From interpreting ECGs to understanding updated pharmacological treatments, ChatGPT serves as a reliable tool for refreshing critical medical knowledge.

10.4 Biometrics in Medicine

Biometrics, the measurement and statistical analysis of physical and biological data, plays a pivotal role in modern medicine by enabling precise definition and diagnosis of illnesses. By leveraging advanced sensors and analytical tools, biometrics provides detailed insights into physiological and pathological states, facilitating more accurate and timely interventions.

Defining Illnesses Through Biometrics

Biometric data is essential in identifying and characterizing diseases, including:

- **Cardiovascular Diseases:** Metrics such as heart rate variability and blood pressure are used to detect and monitor conditions like arrhythmias and hypertension. Devices equipped with photoplethysmography sensors have demonstrated over 95 % accuracy in identifying atrial fibrillation.
- **Respiratory Disorders:** Tools such as spirometry and pulse oximetry measure lung function and oxygen saturation, aiding in the diagnosis of asthma, chronic obstructive pulmonary disease (COPD), and sleep apnea.

- **Diabetes Management:** Continuous glucose monitoring systems track blood sugar levels in real-time, providing critical data for managing diabetes. Advanced devices have reduced hypoglycemic events by 27 % in clinical trials.
- **Infectious Diseases:** Biometrics track symptoms and physiological responses, such as fever and respiratory rate, enabling early detection of infections like COVID-19. AI-integrated wearable devices achieved a 90 % success rate in predicting illness onset during the pandemic.

Biometric technologies are redefining how illnesses are diagnosed and managed, offering personalized, data-driven approaches to healthcare that improve outcomes and efficiency.

10.5 Challenges in Psychiatry: The Absence of Biometric Definitions

While biometrics has transformed the diagnosis of physical illnesses, psychiatry continues to lack comparable markers to define mental health conditions. Unlike diseases such as diabetes or cardiovascular disorders, mental illnesses are primarily diagnosed through subjective evaluations of symptoms and patient interviews.

Subjectivity in Diagnosis

Mental health diagnoses rely on criteria outlined in manuals such as the DSM-5 (see p. 20), which focus on symptom clusters rather than objective biomarkers. This reliance introduces significant variability:

- **Behavioral Assessments:** Conditions like depression and anxiety are diagnosed based on patient-reported experiences and clinician observations, which are influenced by cultural and individual differences.
- **Lack of Standardized Biometrics:** Unlike physical illnesses, psychiatry lacks universally accepted physiological or genetic markers for disorders such as bipolar disorder and schizophrenia.

Efforts to Identify Biometric Markers in Psychiatry

Despite these challenges, researchers are making progress toward identifying reliable biometric markers for mental health conditions. Some promising approaches include:

- **Neuroimaging Studies:** Techniques such as functional MRI (fMRI) and electroencephalography (EEG) have revealed neural activity patterns associated

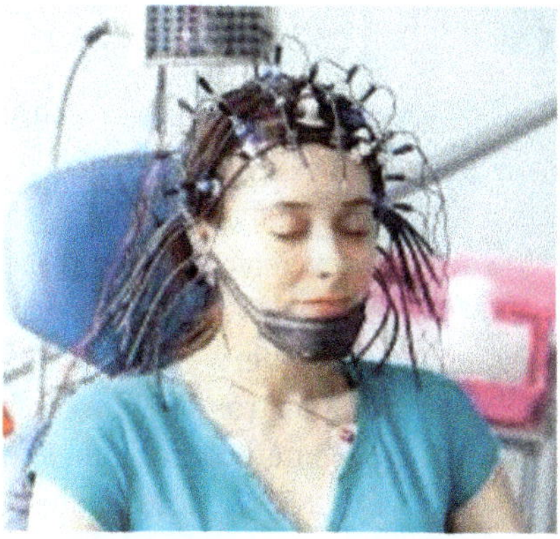

Figure 10.3: EEG in psychiatric research.

with disorders like schizophrenia and Attention-Deficit/Hyperactivity Disorder (ADHD). However, these findings are not yet robust or consistent enough for clinical application.
- **Physiological Metrics:** Metrics such as heart rate variability and cortisol levels have shown potential links to anxiety and stress disorders. However, their diagnostic specificity is limited due to the influence of multiple external and internal factors.

The Path Forward

The absence of biometric definitions in psychiatry highlights the need for innovative, multidisciplinary research that integrates neuroscience, data science, and clinical expertise. Key focus areas include:
- **Advances in AI and Machine Learning:** AI-powered analysis of multimodal data—such as speech patterns, text, and physiological metrics—offers promising pathways for uncovering reliable biomarkers.
- **Longitudinal Studies:** Comprehensive, long-term studies that track patients over time could help identify consistent patterns and markers for psychiatric disorders.
- **Ethical Considerations:** As psychiatry begins to incorporate biometric technologies, safeguarding patient privacy and ensuring equitable access to these advancements will be critical.

While physical medicine benefits from well-defined biometric pathways for diagnosis and treatment, psychiatry remains heavily reliant on subjective measures. This gap underscores the urgent need for continued research and innovation to bridge the divide and improve the accuracy and reliability of psychiatric diagnoses.

10.6 AI in Mental Health Diagnosis

AI algorithms are becoming invaluable in identifying and diagnosing mental health conditions, often matching or surpassing human accuracy:

- **Speech and Text Analysis:** Studies show that AI systems analyzing speech patterns can identify depression with up to 85 % accuracy by detecting changes in tone, pitch, and word choice. For instance, IBM Watson Health has developed a tool that identifies depressive tendencies through patient interviews.
- **Behavioral Data Monitoring:** Smartphone apps like Mindstrong Health track metrics such as typing speed, screen activity, and social interaction frequency. These behavioral markers predict mood changes with a 75 % success rate in identifying early signs of bipolar disorder.
- **Neuroimaging Insights:** AI tools analyzing fMRI scans identify structural and functional abnormalities associated with psychiatric conditions. A Stanford University study reported 88 % accuracy in diagnosing schizophrenia using neural imaging data combined with machine learning algorithms.
- **Social Media and Online Activity:** AI algorithms monitor social media posts and user activity to detect warning signs of mental health issues. A study published in *Nature Human Behaviour* found that analyzing Instagram photos could detect depression with 70 % accuracy based on factors like color tones, brightness, and engagement patterns.

10.7 AI in Mental Health Treatment Planning

AI is enhancing therapeutic interventions by creating personalized treatment strategies tailored to individual needs:

- **Chatbots for CBT[1] (Cognitive Behavioral Therapy):** AI-driven chatbots such as Woebot and Wysa offer accessible mental health support. Clinical trials show that Woebot users experienced a 32 % reduction in anxiety and a 28 % reduction in depressive symptoms over eight weeks. These platforms are particularly valuable in regions with limited access to therapists.
- **Personalized Treatment Plans:** AI platforms like Quartet Health use patient data to match individuals with appropriate therapists or treatment modalities. These systems improve treatment success rates by 24 %, as noted in a 2023 study published in a journal of the American Psychiatric Association.

1 CBT, or Cognitive Behavioral Therapy, is a widely used, evidence-based psychotherapy focusing on identifying and changing negative thought patterns and behaviors that contribute to emotional distress and mental health issues.

- **Predicting Treatment Response:** AI models analyze genetic, clinical, and behavioral data to predict individual responses to antidepressants. For example, a machine learning model developed by Precision Health AI predicts the effectiveness of selective serotonin reuptake inhibitors with 80 % accuracy, enabling clinicians to select optimal medications more efficiently.

10.8 AI and Suicide Prevention

AI is playing a crucial role in addressing suicide, a pressing public health issue:

- **Risk Prediction Models:** Vanderbilt University researchers developed an AI model that analyzes electronic health records to predict suicide attempts with 90 % accuracy within a two-week window.
- **Social Media Monitoring:** Tools like Samaritans Radar analyze social media posts for language patterns indicative of suicidal ideation. A 2021 study found these systems effective in flagging 72 % of high-risk individuals.
- **Crisis Intervention Systems:** AI-powered crisis helplines, such as those used by Crisis Text Line, analyze caller sentiment in real time to prioritize high-risk cases. These systems improve response times by 33 %, enabling timely interventions.
- **Proactive Monitoring:** AI systems integrated with wearable devices monitor physiological data, such as heart rate variability and sleep patterns, to identify stress and suicidal ideation. Fitbit's partnership with mental health researchers demonstrated 85 % accuracy in predicting acute stress episodes.

Figure 10.4: AI and suicide prevention.

Conclusion

AI is reshaping medicine—and psychiatry in particular—by enhancing diagnostic capabilities, personalizing treatment plans, and expanding access to care. By leveraging the power of AI, mental health outcomes can be improved on a global scale, offering hope to millions of individuals worldwide.

11 Education Reimagined

Education is undergoing a profound transformation, driven by the possibilities of Artificial Intelligence (AI). From personalized learning experiences to automated assessments, AI is reshaping how knowledge is delivered, accessed, and evaluated. This chapter examines the innovative ways AI is redefining the educational landscape.

11.1 The Traditional Model

For centuries, education followed a one-size-fits-all model, with students adhering to a structured curriculum within formal institutions. While this approach was instrumental in promoting global literacy and foundational knowledge, it often failed to address the diverse needs of learners. Standardized testing emerged as the dominant measure of success, prioritizing memorization over understanding, creativity, and critical thinking.

Traditional classrooms were constrained by rigid schedules and curriculum requirements, leaving minimal room for individual exploration or personalized attention. High-achieving students often felt unchallenged, while those struggling risked falling behind. Geographic, economic, and resource disparities further amplified these challenges, limiting equal access to quality education.

Figure 11.1: A traditional classroom in the 20th century.

https://doi.org/10.1515/9783111710808-015

Historical Perspective: The industrial revolution gave rise to the modern education system, designed primarily to equip workers with standardized skills for factory jobs. While this system successfully promoted basic literacy and numeracy, it has struggled to adapt to the rapidly changing demands of contemporary society. Today's learners face challenges that require creativity, adaptability, and critical thinking—qualities often overlooked in traditional educational frameworks.

Global Challenges in Education:

- **Equity in Access:** Rural communities and developing nations face significant barriers, including a shortage of trained teachers, inadequate resources, and outdated curricula.
- **Skill Gaps:** Many graduates enter the workforce lacking proficiency in critical areas such as technology, communication, and problem-solving.
- **Mental Health:** High-stakes exams and competitive academic environments contribute to increasing levels of anxiety, stress, and burnout among students.

11.2 Transforming Learning

The emergence of ChatGPT and similar AI technologies marks a paradigm shift in education. By harnessing AI's ability to deliver instant, personalized feedback, and adaptive learning experiences, the focus transitions from standardization to individualization. AI-powered education empowers learners to explore topics at their own pace, revisit challenging concepts, and engage in interactive discussions that enhance comprehension and retention.

Example: Tailored Tutoring Imagine a student struggling with geometry, particularly the Pythagorean theorem. ChatGPT can not only explain the formula but also guide the student through step-by-step problem-solving strategies, provide interactive diagrams, and offer customized practice problems tailored to their learning pace and needs.

Enhanced Classroom Interactions Teachers incorporating ChatGPT in their classrooms report increased student engagement. For example, a biology teacher can use AI to create interactive quizzes or simplify complex processes like DNA replication through animations, analogies, and real-time demonstrations.

Collaborative Learning with AI Group projects are enriched by AI integration. For instance, students collaborating on a history presentation can leverage ChatGPT to draft scripts, suggest innovative visuals, and fact-check sources instantly, streamlining the creative and research processes.

Case Study: A Rural School's Transformation In a remote Kenyan village, a pilot program introduced ChatGPT-enabled tablets in a local school. Within six months, students achieved a remarkable 40 % improvement in math and reading scores, aided by access to personalized learning resources available in both Swahili and English.

11.3 Personalized and Lifelong Learning

Personalized Learning ChatGPT's AI-driven capabilities enable the customization of educational content to suit each user's proficiency level and learning speed. For example:

- **Beginner Level:** A young learner exploring basic science concepts, such as photosynthesis, can benefit from simplified explanations and engaging illustrative examples.
- **Advanced Level:** A college student studying molecular biology can delve into the intricate mechanisms of photosynthesis, complete with references to recent research and advanced analyses.

Lifelong Learning ChatGPT facilitates continuous education beyond traditional academic settings. Adults looking to upskill can learn topics such as coding, financial literacy, or foreign languages. For instance, a professional learning Python can access tailored coding exercises, debugging assistance, and explanations aligned with their expertise level.

Interdisciplinary Exploration AI nurtures curiosity across diverse fields. A high school student passionate about sustainability might explore renewable energy technologies alongside their economic and societal implications. Similarly, ChatGPT can assist professionals investigating interdisciplinary topics, such as the intersection of neuroscience and artificial intelligence.

Learning Through Exploration

ChatGPT fosters exploratory learning by simulating real-world scenarios and engaging users in dynamic, interactive experiences. For example:

- A history student can role-play as a diplomat during the Cold War, using ChatGPT to simulate the decisions and perspectives of key world leaders.
- Aspiring entrepreneurs can receive personalized business strategy guidance, including market analysis, competitive positioning, and actionable recommendations.

11.4 A Global Perspective

AI tools like ChatGPT are transforming education worldwide, breaking down barriers of geography, language, and resources.

Multilingual Education ChatGPT's multilingual capabilities allow students to learn in their native languages while accessing global knowledge. For example:

- A student in rural India can study physics in Hindi and transition seamlessly to English for advanced materials.
- Teachers in under-resourced schools can create lesson plans and activities that align with their students' linguistic and cultural contexts.

Equalizing Opportunities In regions with a shortage of qualified educators, ChatGPT bridges gaps by offering high-quality explanations, practice exercises, and educational resources.

Empowering Refugees and Migrants AI tools are particularly transformative for displaced communities. Refugees with limited access to formal education can use ChatGPT for self-paced learning in mathematics, languages, and vocational skills. For instance, an Afghan refugee preparing for resettlement in Europe can learn German alongside cultural insights, all tailored to their unique needs.

Figure 11.2: Refugees learning English.

11.5 The Educator's Role

In this reimagined educational landscape, the role of educators evolves from being mere dispensers of information to mentors, facilitators, and designers of dynamic learning experiences.

Empowering Educators ChatGPT supports teachers in multiple ways:

- **Lesson Planning:** Generate detailed lesson plans, enabling educators to dedicate more time to engaging with students during class.
- **Grading:** Automate the grading of essays and assignments, allowing teachers to focus on providing meaningful, personalized feedback.
- **Professional Development:** Stay updated on new pedagogical techniques and subject-specific advancements using ChatGPT as a research and training tool.

Blended Learning Models In classrooms, ChatGPT enhances blended learning by offering personalized assistance to students, enabling teachers to concentrate on facilitating discussions, nurturing creativity, and fostering critical thinking.

AI as a Collaborative Partner

When collaborating with ChatGPT, educators can design immersive and engaging learning experiences. For example:

- A history teacher creating a simulation of ancient trade routes can use ChatGPT to script realistic events, design maps, and provide role-playing prompts for students.
- A chemistry instructor can develop real-time virtual lab simulations, ensuring students gain practical experience safely before conducting hands-on experiments.

Case Study: Teacher Collaboration Success At a middle school in California, teachers integrated ChatGPT into project-based learning modules. The results were remarkable: students demonstrated higher engagement and improved problem-solving skills, while educators reported a 25 % reduction in lesson preparation time.

11.6 Conclusion

The reimagined educational landscape, driven by tools like ChatGPT, prioritizes inclusivity, personalization, and lifelong learning. By bridging gaps and unlocking potential, AI is reshaping how we teach and learn, creating a future where education is accessible, equitable, and transformative for all.

Looking Ahead As technology continues to evolve, the integration of AI in education will bring innovative solutions to existing challenges. By adopting these tools responsibly, we can ensure education becomes a universal right—empowering learners worldwide to achieve their fullest potential.

Final Thought Reimagining education with ChatGPT is not just a technological shift but a philosophical transformation. It places the learner at the center of the experience, fostering curiosity, creativity, and a lifelong love of learning.

Figure 11.3: Placing the learner in the center.

12 Business and ChatGPT

The integration of ChatGPT into the business world has revolutionized how companies operate, innovate, and engage with stakeholders. From startups to multinational corporations, ChatGPT drives efficiency, enhances customer interactions, and uncovers new revenue streams. This chapter explores the diverse applications of ChatGPT in the business realm, focusing on its monetization models, role in small businesses, market disruptions, challenges, and transformative impact on global markets.

12.1 AI Monetization Models

ChatGPT's capabilities have paved the way for innovative monetization strategies:

- **Subscription Services:** Businesses leverage ChatGPT through subscription-based platforms offering tiered access to advanced features. For example, professional and enterprise plans provide Application Programming Interfaces (API) integrations, enabling seamless scalability.
- **Customized Solutions:** Companies use ChatGPT's API to develop industry-specific tools, such as financial analysis bots, customer service assistants, and content creation platforms. These tailored solutions often involve licensing fees or revenue-sharing agreements.
- **Pay-Per-Use APIs:** Small businesses can access AI services on a pay-per-use basis, eliminating the need for subscription commitments and reducing upfront costs.
- **Data Insights and Analytics:** ChatGPT analyzes large datasets to provide actionable insights in areas like marketing, product development, and consumer behavior trends, driving informed decision-making.

Case Study: Content Generation Platform A publishing startup integrated ChatGPT into its operations, offering an AI-powered article generation service to clients. By charging clients on a pay-per-use basis, the company scaled rapidly, increasing its customer base by 50 % within the first year.

12.2 ChatGPT in Startups and Small Businesses

Small businesses and startups are leveraging ChatGPT to overcome resource constraints and foster innovation:

https://doi.org/10.1515/9783111710808-016

- **Content Creation:** ChatGPT streamlines the creation of marketing copy and social media posts, saving time and reducing costs for small teams.

Figure 12.1: Drafting marketing copy with ChatGPT.

- **Customer Engagement:** Startups utilize ChatGPT-powered chatbots to handle customer inquiries, improving response times and satisfaction rates while reducing operational overhead.
- **Operational Efficiency:** Administrative tasks such as scheduling, data entry, and invoice generation are streamlined using AI, allowing businesses to focus on core operations.
- **Employee Onboarding:** ChatGPT creates personalized onboarding materials for new employees, enhancing the training experience and saving management time.

Example: ChatGPT-Powered Marketing A fitness studio implemented ChatGPT to generate personalized email campaigns and social media content. The AI tailored messages to different audience segments, resulting in:
- A 25 % increase in membership signups.
- Higher engagement rates across social platforms.
- Significant time savings for the studio's small team.

12.3 Market Disruptions

ChatGPT is not just enhancing existing processes—it is disrupting entire industries by driving innovation and efficiency. Key examples include:

- **E-commerce:** AI-driven product recommendations, virtual shopping assistants, and personalized email campaigns are transforming customer experiences.
- **Real Estate:** ChatGPT assists agents in drafting engaging property descriptions, generating targeted ads, and communicating with clients in multiple languages.
- **Legal Services:** Law firms use ChatGPT to draft contracts, review documents, and research case law, significantly reducing costs and turnaround times.
- **Human Resources:** ChatGPT streamlines recruitment by drafting job descriptions, screening applications, and even conducting preliminary interviews.

Case Study: Real Estate Success A real estate agency integrated ChatGPT into its marketing and client engagement processes. The results included:
- Faster property listings with AI-generated descriptions.
- Improved client satisfaction through automated follow-ups.
- A 15 % increase in property sales over six months.

The Rise of Hyper-Personalization ChatGPT enables hyper-personalization, a key driver of customer loyalty. For instance, e-commerce platforms using AI-generated recommendations reported a 40 % increase in sales conversion rates.

12.4 ChatGPT and Global Markets

As businesses expand globally, ChatGPT plays a pivotal role in bridging linguistic and cultural gaps. Key applications include:
- **Multilingual Communication:** ChatGPT enables businesses to interact with customers in their native languages, increasing engagement and building trust.
- **Localized Marketing:** AI generates region-specific campaigns aligned with local traditions and preferences, ensuring relevance and resonance.
- **Supply Chain Optimization:** ChatGPT analyzes global logistics trends to help companies anticipate disruptions and optimize inventory management.

Case Study: Expanding Internationally A global beauty brand used ChatGPT to localize its marketing campaigns in Europe and Asia. Key outcomes included:
- A 30 % increase in sales in new regions.
- Faster market entry with culturally relevant messaging.
- Improved customer sentiment through native-language support.

12.5 Future Trends

As AI technology evolves, ChatGPT is poised to shape the future of business through emerging trends:

- **Predictive Insights:** ChatGPT will advance in providing predictive analytics, enabling businesses to forecast trends and customer behaviors with greater precision.
- **Autonomous Decision-Making:** AI will take on strategic roles, such as optimizing pricing strategies and identifying growth opportunities.
- **Integration with AR/VR:** ChatGPT-powered virtual assistants will enhance AR/VR experiences, including interactive product demonstrations and immersive customer support.

Example: Predictive Marketing A fashion retailer integrated ChatGPT with its CRM system to predict seasonal demand for clothing items. Results included:

- A 20 % reduction in inventory waste.
- Increased sales through targeted pre-season campaigns.

12.6 Challenges and Ethical Considerations

While the benefits of ChatGPT are transformative, businesses must address key challenges:

- **Data Privacy:** Ensuring compliance with global data protection regulations, such as GDPR (see p. 82).
- **Bias Mitigation:** Reducing biases in AI outputs to promote fairness and inclusivity.
- **Workforce Impact:** Balancing automation with human oversight and reskilling employees.

Actionable Strategies To address these challenges, businesses should:

- Conduct regular AI audits to identify and mitigate biases.
- Train employees to collaborate effectively with AI tools, fostering a synergistic approach.
- Implement transparent data-handling policies to build and maintain customer trust.

12.7 Conclusion

The adoption of ChatGPT in business represents a fundamental shift in how companies operate and create value. By streamlining processes, enhancing customer experiences, and unlocking new revenue streams, ChatGPT has become indispensable in the digital age.

Looking Ahead: Businesses that responsibly embrace ChatGPT's potential will maintain a competitive edge in an ever-evolving market. The path forward lies not only in adopting AI but in leveraging it to inspire creativity, foster inclusivity, and drive sustainable growth.

Figure 12.2: Using ChatGPT responsibly.

Part V: **Beyond ChatGPT**

13 Tesla FSD

Figure 13.1: Tesla Model S.

I purchased my first Tesla Model S in early 2016. At that time, the *self-driving* feature was powered by Mobileye, an Israeli company. By the time I upgraded to my second Tesla Model S in 2021, Tesla had long moved past Mobileye, having developed its own autonomous driving system. Currently, this system is branded as FSD[1] Supervised.

13.1 Introduction

In early 2004, Elon Musk led Tesla Motors' initial Series A funding round, contributing $6.5 million of the $7.5 million raised and joining the company's board of directors as chairman.

Tesla was founded in 2003 by Martin Eberhard and Marc Tarpenning. Musk's significant financial investment and his vision for sustainable transportation quickly positioned him as the face and driving force behind the company.

Through strategic vision and engineering expertise, Musk propelled Tesla from a fledgling startup to a global leader in electric vehicles and renewable energy. Under his leadership, Tesla expanded its product line, innovated in battery technology, and consistently pushed the boundaries of what electric vehicles could achieve, cementing his critical role in the company's success.

1 FSD is an advanced driver-assistance system (ADAS) designed to enable vehicles to drive themselves under most or all conditions, with minimal or no human intervention. It is typically associated with Tesla's suite of autonomous driving features.

https://doi.org/10.1515/9783111710808-018

13.2 Tesla's Full Self-Driving (FSD) Technology

Development History

Tesla's autonomous journey began in 2014 with *Autopilot*, offering semi-autonomous features like lane-keeping and adaptive cruise control. These capabilities evolved through OTA (Over-The-Air) updates, showcasing Tesla's iterative approach. In 2016, Tesla announced its vision for a fully self-driving car. By 2019, the company began rolling out the FSD (see p. 111) package, promising advanced autonomous features.

Tesla's vertical integration—designing both hardware and software in-house—has accelerated innovation. The company leverages data from millions of miles driven by its vehicles to refine its algorithms, making continuous advancements possible.

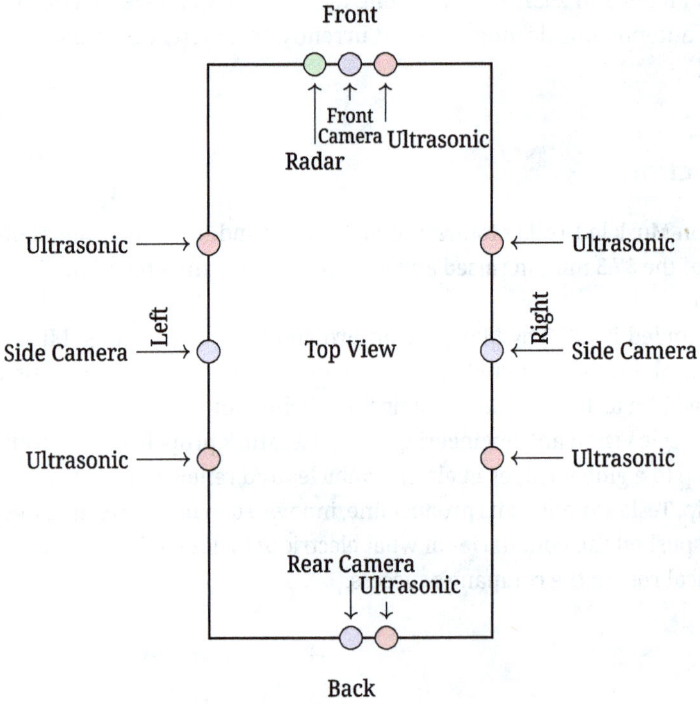

Figure 13.2: FSD (see p. 111) sensor layout on a Tesla vehicle. Blue circles represent cameras, green circles represent radar, and red circles represent ultrasonic sensors.

User Engagement and Feedback System

Tesla's FSD (see p. 111) Beta program relies heavily on feedback from users who test pre-release features on public roads. This allows Tesla to gather data on system performance in real-world conditions, enabling refinement of its algorithms and ensuring the technology remains adaptive and safe.

Future Innovations in Tesla FSD

Looking ahead, Tesla envisions deeper integration with smart city infrastructure. Real-time communication between Tesla vehicles and connected road systems could optimize traffic flow and enable more seamless navigation, particularly in urban environments.

13.3 Ethical Frameworks and Challenges

Comparison of Ethical Frameworks

Tesla's ethical approach to autonomous driving decisions, including life-critical scenarios like the *trolley problem*, is often compared to frameworks adopted by competitors. For example, Waymo emphasizes scenario-specific risk mitigation, while Tesla's data-driven approach relies on real-world learning to refine decision-making in complex situations. Ethical standards such as the IEEE Global Initiative on Ethics of Autonomous and Intelligent Systems serve as benchmarks for ensuring responsible AI deployment.

Climate Impact Metrics

Tesla's FSD (see p. 111), combined with its all-electric fleet, is a cornerstone of its environmental mission. Optimized routes, reduced traffic congestion, and energy-efficient driving all contribute to a significant reduction in greenhouse gas emissions, aligning with global sustainability goals.

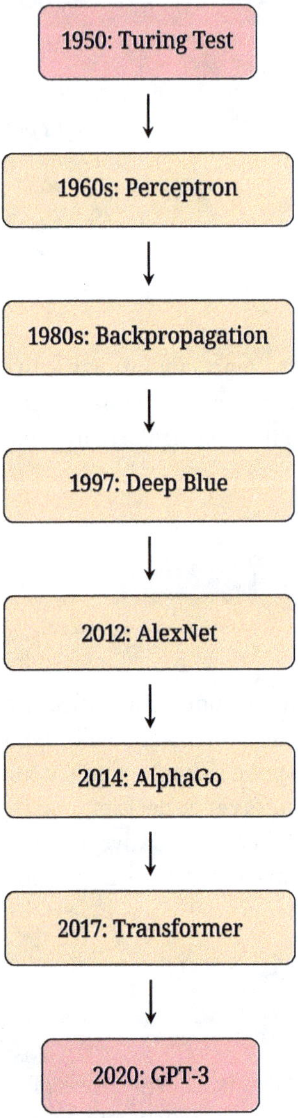

Figure 13.3: Timeline of key milestones in Tesla's FSD (see p. 111) development.

13.4 Market Analysis

Expanded Competitor Analysis

Tesla faces strong competition from Waymo, which employs LiDAR[2] alongside radar and cameras for high precision. Cruise, meanwhile, focuses on urban driving scenarios. Tesla's camera-based approach stands out for its cost-effectiveness, fleet-scale learning, and OTA capabilities, allowing for rapid updates that competitors may struggle to match.

Public Perception Through Media

Media coverage plays a pivotal role in shaping public trust in FSD (see p. 111). While Tesla's innovations receive praise, incidents involving FSD-equipped vehicles often dominate headlines, underscoring the need for transparent communication and ongoing safety improvements.

13.5 Technical Challenges and Innovations

Addressing Skepticism

Despite significant advancements, challenges like phantom braking and the interpretation of complex traffic scenarios persist. Tesla's OTA updates aim to address these concerns iteratively, reinforcing public trust through transparency and consistent improvements.

Sensor Technology and Data Processing

Tesla's reliance on cameras instead of LiDAR remains a point of contention. However, the development of the Full Self-Driving Computer (Hardware 3) and advanced neural networks allows Tesla to maximize the potential of its vision-based system, ensuring high levels of safety and accuracy.

---

2 LiDAR stands for Light Detection and Ranging. It is a remote sensing method that uses light in the form of a pulsed laser to measure variable distances to the Earth or other objects. These light pulses, combined with other data recorded by the system, generate precise, three-dimensional information about the shape of the Earth and its surface characteristics.

Figure 13.4: Sensor technology.

13.6 Impact on Society and Urban Infrastructure

Socio-Economic Implications

The adoption of FSD (see p. 111) technology will transform industries and challenge traditional job markets, particularly for drivers. However, new opportunities in AI development and autonomous systems management will emerge. Tesla is also exploring mobility solutions for the elderly and disabled, improving accessibility and social inclusion.

Urban Planning and Infrastructure

Cities may need to adapt their infrastructure for autonomous vehicles by redesigning intersections, implementing smart traffic management systems, and creating dedicated lanes. Tesla's vision of shared autonomous vehicles could reduce parking space demand and promote sustainable urban design.

13.7 Conclusion

Tesla's FSD (see p. 111) technology represents the forefront of autonomous driving, blending innovative hardware, AI-driven software, and extensive real-world data collection. While significant technical and ethical challenges remain, Tesla's iterative approach and commitment to sustainability place it in a strong position to redefine transportation.

Through a combination of technological advancement and public engagement, Tesla's FSD (see p. 111) system holds the potential to transform mobility, improve safety, and reduce environmental impact. As this technology continues to evolve, it is set to play a pivotal role in shaping the future of transportation.

14 Alibaba

Figure 14.1: Alibaba and the Forty Thieves.

I shop mostly on Amazon. As an individual, I do not buy wholesale—LOL—and that's primarily what Alibaba provides. Is Alibaba bigger than Amazon? If we consider each marketplace's retail market share in their home countries, then yes, Alibaba is bigger. For example, while Amazon's retail share in the US market is nearly 50 %, Alibaba's share in China reaches 80 %. Impressive!

My attention was drawn to Alibaba by a 2024 news article about Jack Ma, the legendary executive chairman of Alibaba, and his address at an AI conference. He shared how Alibaba provides ChatGPT-like services to over 200,000 suppliers. Truly, this is "Beyond ChatGPT".

The name Alibaba came from a brainstorming session. Jack Ma was in a San Francisco coffee shop when he thought of the name. He asked the waitress if it sounded familiar.

"I said, 'What do you know about Alibaba?' and she said, 'Open Sesame.' And I said, 'Yes, this is the name!'" he told the interviewer. In the story, the phrase *Open Sesame* magically opens a treasure-filled cave.

Ma liked the name because "Alibaba is a kind, smart business person, and he helped the village," he explained. "Alibaba opens sesame for small- to medium-sized companies."

They even trademarked *Alimama*, in case someone wanted to 'marry' Alibaba.

https://doi.org/10.1515/9783111710808-019

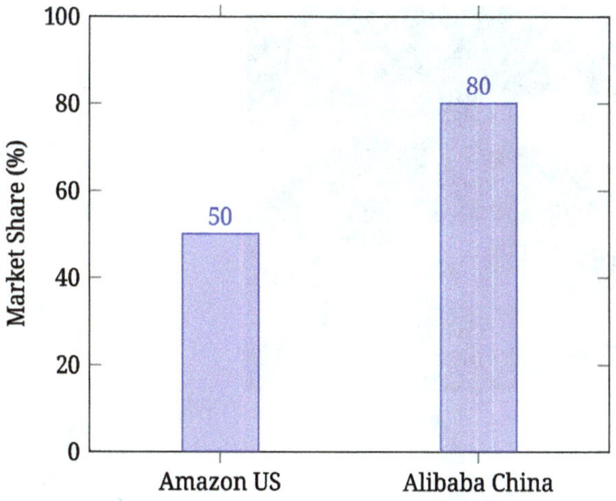

Figure 14.2: Market share comparison: Amazon vs. Alibaba.

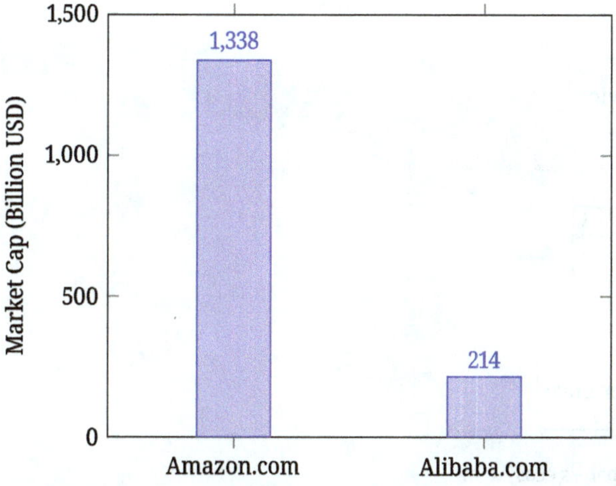

Figure 14.3: Market capitalization: Amazon vs. Alibaba.

14.1 AI Strategy

Overview Alibaba, one of the world's largest e-commerce companies, has strategically integrated AI into its ecosystem. This approach leverages advanced technologies to streamline operations and enhance efficiency.

At the core of Alibaba's AI strategy is its data-centric approach. This enables the company to predict consumer behavior, manage inventory, and personalize customer experiences effectively.

Figure 14.4: Jack Ma.

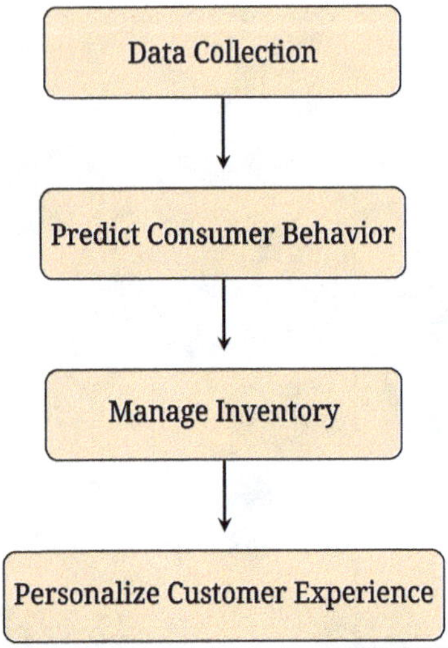

Figure 14.5: AI integration in Alibaba's ecosystem.

Objectives Alibaba uses AI to achieve several key goals:

- **Enhancing Customer Experience:** Personalizing shopping experiences boosts customer satisfaction, sales, and loyalty.
- **Optimizing Logistics:** Predictive analytics optimize delivery routes, inventory, and demand forecasting.
- **Improving Efficiency:** Routine tasks are automated, allowing employees to focus on strategic activities.
- **Driving Innovation:** Continuous R&D ensures Alibaba remains at the cutting edge of AI technology.

- **Ensuring Security:** AI systems comply with global data protection regulations, fostering trust and compliance.

14.2 AI for Sustainability

Alibaba leverages AI to optimize energy use in its data centers and logistics operations. By integrating AI-powered route planning and demand prediction, the company minimizes fuel consumption and reduces greenhouse gas emissions.

Smart Warehousing AI automates warehouse operations, reducing energy waste and improving efficiency.

Green Supply Chain AI-driven insights help suppliers adopt sustainable practices, such as efficient packaging and eco-friendly materials.

Carbon Tracking Alibaba tracks its carbon emissions using AI and has committed to achieving carbon neutrality in its operations by 2030.

14.3 Future AI Innovations at Alibaba

Alibaba envisions expanding its AI capabilities with cutting-edge technologies. Upcoming initiatives include:

- **Quantum Computing:** Research into quantum algorithms aims to revolutionize data processing for logistics and predictive analytics.
- **Metaverse Commerce:** Using AI, Alibaba is developing immersive shopping experiences in the metaverse to engage consumers in new ways.
- **Blockchain Integration:** Combining AI with blockchain ensures secure and transparent transactions, enhancing trust in digital marketplaces.

14.4 Challenges and Ethical Considerations

While AI offers immense potential, it also presents challenges:

- **Bias in Algorithms:** Ensuring fairness and avoiding bias in AI models is critical to building consumer trust.
- **Data Privacy:** As a global leader, Alibaba must comply with varying data protection regulations across regions.
- **Job Displacement:** Automation may impact traditional jobs. Alibaba addresses this through reskilling programs for affected employees.

To mitigate these challenges, Alibaba emphasizes ethical AI use and transparent practices, fostering collaboration with policymakers and stakeholders worldwide.

14.5 Global AI Success Stories

Europe

In Europe, Alibaba's AI-powered marketing tools enabled small businesses to access large consumer bases. One supplier reported a 30 % increase in cross-border sales by leveraging personalized ad campaigns.

South Asia

In India, Alibaba's AI logistics solutions helped reduce delivery times by 40 %, significantly improving customer satisfaction and retention rates.

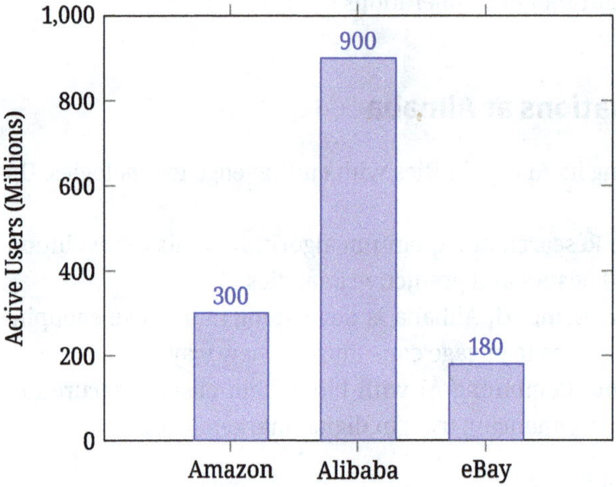

Figure 14.6: Active user comparison across platforms.

Part VI: **The Future**

15 Future Applications of ChatGPT

The future of ChatGPT lies in its potential to redefine industries, empower innovation, and create entirely new use cases. This chapter explores some of the most promising applications on the horizon.

15.1 AI in Virtual and Augmented Reality

Imagine a world where ChatGPT interacts with users in immersive environments. Applications include:

Virtual Tutors: ChatGPT guiding students through simulations, such as historical reenactments or scientific experiments.

Gaming: Dynamic, AI-generated Non-Player Character (NPC) dialogues that evolve based on player actions.

Example: A VR game where NPCs, powered by ChatGPT, offer personalized quests and responses. Challenges: Integration of real-time AI with rendering engines requires significant computational resources.

15.2 Healthcare Integration

AI-assisted healthcare will benefit from ChatGPT in these ways:

Diagnostic Assistance: AI interpreting patient data and suggesting diagnoses.

Therapeutic Applications: ChatGPT-powered mental health tools for CBT (see p. 94).

Example: ChatGPT guiding patients through stress management exercises, tailored to individual needs.

Ethical Considerations: Ensuring patient data privacy and addressing biases in medical recommendations.

15.3 Future of Customer Support

ChatGPT will redefine customer support:
- Real-time sentiment analysis to tailor interactions.
- Handling complex queries through multi-turn conversations.

Example: ChatGPT integrated into call centers, reducing response times by 30 %.

Limitations: Maintaining human oversight for high-stakes interactions.

https://doi.org/10.1515/9783111710808-021

15.4 Beyond Text: Multimodal AI

The evolution of ChatGPT into a multimodal AI system could include capabilities such as:
- Analyzing images or videos.
- Generating audio responses.

Example: A ChatGPT-powered app offering both text and visual cooking instructions for users with disabilities.

Figure 15.1: Multimodal AI.

15.5 Conclusion: The Path Ahead

While promising, the future of ChatGPT hinges on addressing ethical and technical challenges. Collaborative efforts between developers, users, and regulators will shape its trajectory.

The 12 days of OpenAI, Dec. 9–Dec. 20, 2024.

OpenAI's "12 Days of Shipmas" event, featured daily announcements of new AI features and tools. Below is a summary of the key developments:

On Day 1, OpenAI introduced the o1 reasoning model, a faster and more accurate AI system, alongside ChatGPT Pro, a $200-per-month subscription offering access to advanced models like o1, o1-mini, GPT-4o, and Advanced Voice Mode.

Day 2 focused on developers with an expansion of the "Reinforcement Fine-Tuning Research Program," enabling domain-specific expert models with minimal training data.

Day 3 saw the release of Sora, OpenAI's video generation model, which allows users to create videos from text or images and includes a storyboard feature for greater precision.

On Day 4, OpenAI launched Canvas, a collaborative tool integrated into ChatGPT that provides an editable side panel for writing and coding tasks.

Day 5 featured integration with Apple Intelligence, enhancing Siri with ChatGPT responses across Apple's platforms.

Day 6 introduced Advanced Voice with Video, which pairs ChatGPT's voice capabilities with video generation, as well as a Santa Mode for seasonal interactions.

On Day 7, "Projects" was added to ChatGPT, enabling users to upload files, organize conversations, and set custom instructions for improved workflow management.

Day 8 unveiled ChatGPT Search, a tool for retrieving answers from web sources, first introduced in October 2024, optimized for speed and relevance.

Day 9 highlighted OpenAI o1 and new tools for developers, including Real-time API improvements and a new fine-tuning method for creating specialized AI solutions.

On Day 10, OpenAI launched a feature allowing users to call ChatGPT for up to 15 minutes for free via a designated phone number.

Day 11 focused on working with apps, enabling ChatGPT to integrate and function seamlessly across multiple applications.

Finally, on Day 12, OpenAI previewed its o3 and o3-mini models, expected to launch publicly in early 2025, showcasing advancements in AI reasoning and interaction.

15.6 Alice and the Red Queen

In *Through the Looking-Glass, and What Alice Found There* (Macmillan, 1871), Lewis Carroll recounts the Red Queen's famous words to Alice: "Now, here, you see, it takes all the running you can do, to keep in the same place. If you want to get somewhere else, you must run at least twice as fast as that!"

Is this a metaphor for the rapid progress of AI today? How can one possibly write a book about a subject that evolves so quickly?

Figure 15.2: Alice and the Red Queen.

For instance, as I write this, 'ChatGPT Scheduled Task' is only three days old—it is a remarkably useful new feature. Here's an example of how it works:

I describe my stock portfolio to ChatGPT:

> My Portfolio: I have 100 shares of Apple and 200 shares of Tesla.

Then, using ChatGPT Scheduled Task, I instruct:

> Every workday at 10 AM, noon, and 4 PM, send me a text with the value of my portfolio.

Here's another task:

> Every workday at 4 PM, send me a text: Pick up your daughter at school.

So, how can one write a book on a subject that changes so rapidly?

The answer is that while ChatGPT is indeed becoming more capable by the day, this book focuses on principles and goals that remain constant: writing effective prompts, engaging in meaningful conversations with ChatGPT, and understanding its broad applications in everyday life, education, healthcare, and beyond.

Once you master these foundational skills and "run at least twice as fast," you will always stay ahead.

Have fun.

Part VII: **Two More Things...**

16 Limitations

Figure 16.1: Steve Jobs: *One more thing....*

Steve Jobs' iconic phrase, *One more thing...* marked the moment he unveiled a product just when the audience thought the event was over. (See Macworld, July 23, 2020, for a complete compilation.) In this Part, we introduce two additional important chapters—just when you thought it was all over.

16.1 Common AI Errors

While ChatGPT is a powerful tool, it is essential to understand its limitations to use it effectively. This section discusses common AI errors, their broader implications, and strategies for mitigating their impact.

Hallucinations

Description: AI-generated content that is nonsensical or factually incorrect. Occurs when the AI produces plausible-sounding but inaccurate information.
Example: Summarizing a novel with details that do not exist in the actual text.
Impact: Can mislead users and undermine trust in AI tools.

Lack of Contextual Understanding

Description: AI may fail to grasp the full context of a conversation or prompt, leading to irrelevant or inappropriate responses.
Example: Providing a generic answer when specific details are required.

https://doi.org/10.1515/9783111710808-023

Impact: Reduces user satisfaction, especially in domains requiring nuanced understanding.

Repetition and Redundancy

Description: AI can repeat itself or provide redundant information, particularly in longer interactions.
Example: Offering multiple variations of the same point in a detailed explanation.
Impact: Wastes time and can frustrate users in extended sessions.

Bias in Responses

Description: AI might produce biased content, reflecting biases present in its training data.
Example: Responses unintentionally favoring certain viewpoints or stereotypes.
Impact: May perpetuate or amplify social biases, leading to ethical concerns.

Misinterpretation of Prompts

Description: The AI may misunderstand the intent behind a prompt, leading to irrelevant or incorrect answers.
Example: Misinterpreting a technical question as a request for general information.
Impact: Reduces the effectiveness of AI for specialized or nuanced tasks.

16.2 Broader Implications of Errors

Business Impact

Errors in AI responses can lead to customer dissatisfaction, financial losses, and damage to brand reputation.

Academic Challenges

Misleading information can disrupt research, hinder learning, and propagate inaccuracies.

Public Perception

High-profile AI errors can erode trust in technology, making adoption of AI tools more challenging.

16.3 Strategies for Mitigating AI Errors

Recognizing AI Errors

- **Cross-Verification:** Always verify the information provided by AI against reliable sources.
- **Critical Evaluation:** Assess coherence and plausibility; if something seems off, it likely is.
- **Contextual Consistency:** Ensure AI responses align with the provided context.
- **Checking for Redundancy:** Watch for repetitive information, which may signal misunderstanding.

Crafting Clear Prompts

- **Specificity:** Be as specific as possible in prompts to reduce ambiguity.
- **Step-by-Step Instructions:** Break down complex queries into smaller, manageable parts.

Iterative Refinement

- **Refinement:** If the initial response is unsatisfactory, refine your prompt and ask follow-up questions.
- **Conversation Management:** Use AI responses to guide subsequent queries effectively.

Utilizing Expert Models

- **Specialized GPTs:** Use models fine-tuned for specific tasks or domains.
- **Context Setting:** Begin with a prompt specifying the domain, such as *“Be an expert on 20th-century novels.”*

Post-Processing and Editing

- **Manual Review:** Always review and edit AI-generated content before use.
- **Supplementary Tools:** Use tools for grammar and style checking to refine output further.

Feedback and Learning

- **Providing Feedback:** Use AI feedback mechanisms to report inaccuracies or issues.
- **Continuous Learning:** Stay updated on new features and best practices.

16.4 Effective Prompt Refinement

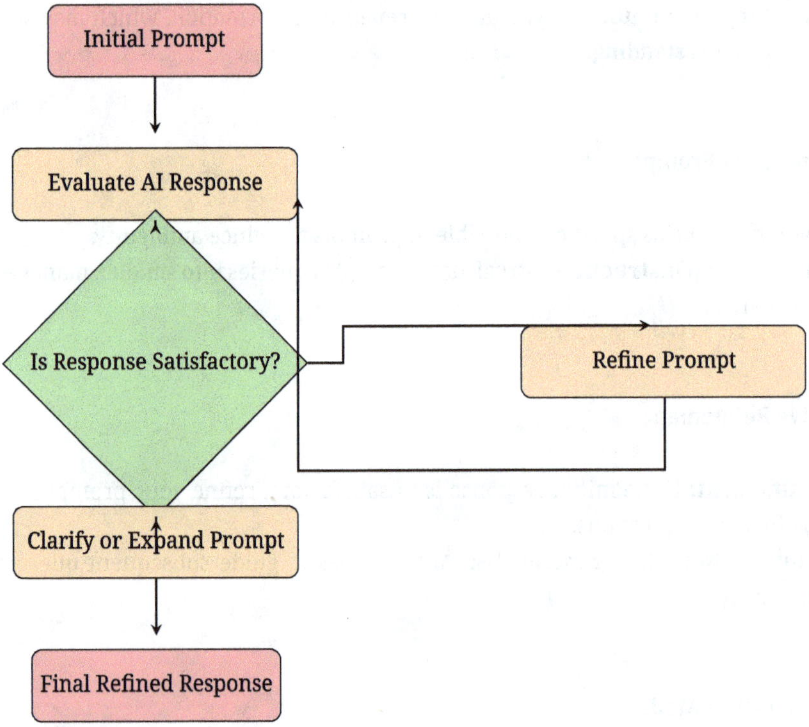

Figure 16.2: Prompt refinement.

Improving prompt clarity and specificity leads to more accurate responses. Examples:

Refine

Explain the Pythagorean theorem.

The Pythagorean theorem states that in a right-angled triangle, the square of the hypotenuse equals the sum of the squares of the other two sides.

Explain the Pythagorean theorem and its significance in geometry.

The Pythagorean theorem is a principle in geometry stating that in a right-angled triangle, the hypotenuse squared equals the sum of the squares of the other two sides. It is significant in fields like trigonometry, physics, and engineering.

Step-by-Step Instructions

How do you solve a quadratic equation?

Better:

Explain the step-by-step process of solving a quadratic equation using factoring.

Steps:
1. Ensure the equation is in $ax^2 + bx + c = 0$ form.
2. Identify two numbers that multiply to ac and add to b.
3. Rewrite the middle term using these numbers.
4. Factor by grouping.
5. Solve for x by setting factors to zero.

16.5 Tokens, Darn It

ChatGPT uses tokens to measure the size of prompts and responses, with a limit of approximately 8,000 tokens (roughly 12 pages of text). To manage token limits:
- Draft concise prompts.

Figure 16.3: Tokens.

- Use specific prompts to focus responses.
- Extract only essential parts of lengthy inputs.

16.6 Conclusions

By addressing limitations and leveraging effective strategies, users can maximize the potential of ChatGPT while minimizing its shortcomings. Continuous learning, ethical considerations, and effective prompt engineering are key to responsible and impactful AI usage.

Guiding with soft words,
Simple things bring peace and joy—
Gentle heart, clear mind.

In the future's hands,
Tools of light and thought will shape
Dreams into new worlds.

ChatGPT

17 Can You Catch the Cheaters?

Did ChatGPT write this book, or did I? I asked OpenAI's Guardian of the Faith (GPT Output Detector), and it responded: With a 99.98 % probability, it is real. That's good enough for me.

17.1 Introduction

Imagine reading a breaking news article only to find out that it was entirely written by a machine. This scenario is becoming increasingly common as AI technology advances, particularly in natural language processing. With AI models like OpenAI's GPT-4 producing text that is nearly indistinguishable from human writing, differentiating between human and AI-generated content has never been more critical.

Figure 17.1: Cheater 1.

AI's ability to produce high-quality, coherent text at scale makes it highly appealing. However, the potential misuse of AI-generated text introduces risks such as spreading misinformation and compromising academic integrity.

Accurately identifying AI-generated writing is essential to maintain trust across journalism, academia, and online platforms. In this chapter, we explore the telltale signs of AI-generated text, review detection tools, and discuss countermeasures to address these challenges. We also delve into ethical considerations, real-world applications, and future trends in AI text detection.

https://doi.org/10.1515/9783111710808-024

17.2 Detection

How to Detect

How do you detect AI-generated text? Look for these telltale signs:
- **Verbose and Repetitive:** AI-generated text often overexplains concepts and repeats information, sometimes with small variations.
- **Uniform Style:** Unlike human writing, which varies in tone and style, AI text tends to maintain a steady, predictable flow.
- **Repetition of Phrases:** AI models may reuse phrases or ideas, especially in longer texts.
- **Lack of Personal Experience:** AI lacks personal anecdotes, emotions, or unique perspectives that human writers naturally provide.
- **Inconsistent Formality:** Depending on the training data, AI text might be overly formal or too casual for the intended context.
- **Misinterpretation of Context:** AI may misunderstand nuances, leading to responses that feel irrelevant or inappropriate.
- **Pronoun and Perspective Inconsistencies:** AI might switch between perspectives (e. g., first-person to third-person) without clear justification.
- **Formulaic Expressions:** AI-generated text often relies on templates and predictable patterns, lacking the creativity and originality of human writing.
- **Abrupt Topic Shifts:** AI might jump between unrelated ideas without proper transitions, creating unnatural flow.

Detection Tools

As AI-generated text becomes more sophisticated, detection tools must evolve. Current solutions analyze structural, stylistic, and contextual features to differentiate AI-generated content from human writing.

Key AI detection tools include:
- **GPT-2 Output Detector:** Developed by OpenAI, this tool analyzes patterns typical of GPT-2-generated text.
  Analogy: Think of it as a handwriting expert identifying subtle traits unique to a suspect's writing.
- **OpenAI's Text Classifier:** Designed to identify text written by GPT-3 or GPT-4, this classifier detects subtle stylistic differences.
  Analogy: Imagine a master chef distinguishing between a professionally cooked dish and an amateur attempt based on subtle flavors and presentation.
- **GROVER Detector:** A dual-purpose tool that can generate and detect AI-written content, making it invaluable in combating misinformation.
  Analogy: Like a seasoned forger who is also skilled at spotting counterfeit documents.

Figure 17.2: Cheater 2.

While plagiarism detection tools like **Turnitin** and **Grammarly** aren't AI-specific, they can flag unusual patterns and repetitive phrasing often found in AI-generated text.

Linguistic Analysis

Linguistic analysis focuses on structural and stylistic elements. Techniques include:

- **Syntax and Grammar Checking:** AI-generated text often adheres strictly to grammatical rules, but may lack the natural flow of human writing.
- **Stylometric Analysis:** Examines word choice, sentence structure, and punctuation to identify distinctive stylistic fingerprints.

  Analogy: Like matching fingerprints to identify a person, stylometry identifies writing patterns to uncover authorship.
- **Sentiment Analysis:** Measures the emotional tone of text to detect inconsistencies or unnatural expressions.

  Analogy: A digital mood ring revealing the emotional temperature of the text.

Behavioral Analysis

Behavioral analysis focuses on patterns in how text is created:
- **Typing Dynamics:** Human typing often includes variability, pauses, and errors, while AI-generated text is instant and error-free.
- **Editing Patterns:** Human writing undergoes multiple drafts and edits, whereas AI generates polished text in one attempt.
- **Time Analysis:** Humans take significantly longer to write complex content compared to the near-instantaneous output of AI.

17.3 Challenges in Detection

Detecting AI-generated text is becoming increasingly difficult due to advancements in AI models.

Key challenges include:

Improved Language Models

Modern AI models like GPT-4 produce text that closely mimics human nuances, making detection harder.

Transformer Architecture

Transformers, with their self-attention mechanisms, enable AI to understand context with remarkable accuracy, reducing obvious errors.

Neural Network Analysis

Advanced models like BERT (see p. 4) and RoBERTa excel at understanding linguistic subtleties, complicating traditional detection methods.

17.4 Ethical Considerations

The rise of AI-generated text raises critical ethical questions:
- **Accountability:** Establishing clear guidelines for AI usage ensures accountability in content creation.

- **Intellectual Property:** Ownership of AI-generated text is legally ambiguous, necessitating clear policies.
- **Misinformation Risks:** AI can be weaponized to spread false information, emphasizing the need for robust detection tools and public awareness.

Case Study: The 2020 AI News Article

An AI-generated article published by a major news outlet went viral, later revealing subtle inaccuracies and biases. This incident highlighted the potential for AI to disseminate misinformation and underscored the importance of transparency in AI-authored content.

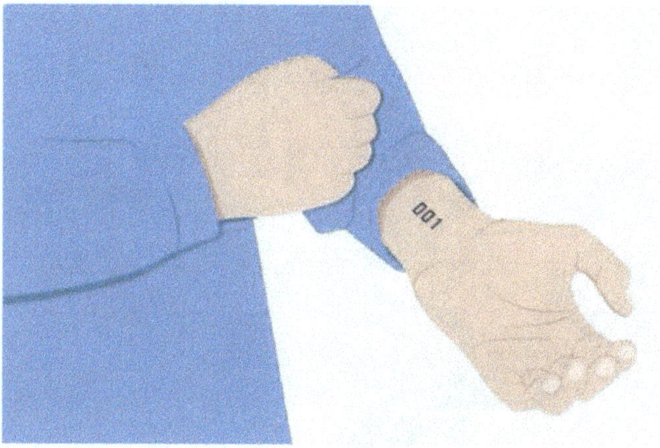

Figure 17.3: Cheater 3.

17.5 Future Trends

Emerging trends in AI detection include:
- **Hybrid Models:** Combining linguistic, behavioral, and machine learning techniques for greater accuracy.
- **Blockchain Verification:** Recording content origins on an immutable ledger to verify authenticity.
- **XAI (Explainable AI):** Offering transparent explanations for why text was flagged as AI-generated.
- **Semantic Analysis:** Understanding the meaning behind text, not just its structure.

17.6 Conclusion

The rise of AI-generated text presents opportunities and challenges. By leveraging advanced detection methods and fostering ethical AI practices, we can preserve the integrity of written content.

17.7 Very Final Conclusion

Can You Catch the Cheaters? Probably not. But we can try.

Glossary

A

Artificial Intelligence (AI): A branch of computer science focused on creating systems capable of performing tasks that typically require human intelligence, such as learning, reasoning, problem-solving, and language understanding.

Attention Mechanism: A method used in transformer models to weigh the importance of different words in a sentence relative to each other.

B

Bias Audits: Regular evaluations conducted to identify and address biases in AI systems, ensuring fairness and equitable treatment across different demographics.

Blockchain Technology: A decentralized and immutable ledger system used to securely store and verify information. In the context of AI, it helps trace and verify the origins of generated content.

C

Case Study: An in-depth analysis of a particular instance, event, or example within a real-world context.

ChatGPT: An AI language model developed by OpenAI, capable of generating coherent and contextually relevant text based on the input it receives.

D

Data Anonymization: Techniques used to remove or obscure personal identifiers from datasets to protect individual privacy.

Deep Learning: A subset of machine learning involving neural networks with many layers, allowing the model to learn complex patterns in large amounts of data.

E

Ethical AI: The practice of designing and deploying AI systems in a manner that ensures fairness, accountability, and transparency.

F

Feature Engineering: The process of selecting, modifying, or creating new input features for machine learning models to improve performance.

Fine-Tuning: The process of adjusting a pre-trained AI model on a narrower dataset to refine its performance for specific applications.

G

Generative Pre-trained Transformer (GPT): A type of AI model based on the transformer architecture, used for generating natural language text.

https://doi.org/10.1515/9783111710808-025

H

Hallucinations: In the context of AI, refers to the generation of incorrect or nonsensical text by the model.

Hyperparameters: Configurable parameters in machine learning models that are set before training begins.

I

Inference: The process by which an AI model generates predictions or outputs based on input data.

Imbalanced Dataset: A dataset where certain classes or categories are underrepresented, leading to biased model predictions.

L

Language Model: A statistical model that predicts the next word in a sequence given the previous words, used in tasks like text generation and speech recognition.

Loss Function: A mathematical function that measures the error of a model's predictions during training.

M

Model Training: The process of teaching an AI model to perform a task by exposing it to data and adjusting its parameters.

N

Neural Networks: Computational models inspired by the human brain, consisting of interconnected nodes (neurons) that process input data to generate output.

O

Overfitting: A modeling error where an AI model learns the training data too well, including noise, reducing its performance on unseen data.

Optimization Algorithm: A mathematical method used to adjust the parameters of a model during training to minimize error.

P

Pretraining: The initial phase of training an AI model on a large corpus of text data.

Prompt Engineering: The practice of crafting effective input prompts to optimize the quality of AI-generated outputs.

R

Reinforcement Learning: A type of machine learning where an agent learns to make decisions by performing actions and receiving rewards or penalties.

Robustness: The ability of an AI system to perform well under varied conditions.

S

Self-Attention: A mechanism in transformers that weighs the importance of different parts of a sentence relative to one another.

Supervised Learning: A type of machine learning where the model is trained on labeled data.

T

Tokenization: The process of breaking down text into smaller units, like words or characters.

Transfer Learning: Adapting a pretrained model for a new but related task.

U

Unsupervised Learning: Machine learning where the model is trained on unlabeled data to discover patterns.

User Consent: Ensuring users are informed about how their data will be used and obtaining explicit permission.

V

Validation Set: A subset of data used to tune the hyperparameters of a model and evaluate its performance.

Voice Recognition: AI systems capable of interpreting and processing spoken language.

Z

Zero-Shot Learning: An AI's ability to perform a task it hasn't been explicitly trained on by leveraging general knowledge.

Bibliography

[1] Bender, E. M., Gebru, T., McMillan-Major, A., & Shmitchell, S. (2021). *On the Dangers of Stochastic Parrots: Can Language Models Be Too Big?*. Proceedings of the 2021 ACM Conference on Fairness, Accountability, and Transparency (FAccT), 610–623.
Summary: Examines the risks of large language models like GPT, including biases and ethical concerns. Discusses the environmental and social impacts of training massive AI systems. Advocates for transparency and responsible deployment of language models.

[2] Bommasani, R., Hudson, D. A., Adcock, A., et al. (2021). *On the Opportunities and Risks of Foundation Models*.
Summary: Analyzes the transformative potential of foundation models like GPT across disciplines. Highlights the risks of misuse, biases, and ethical dilemmas in deploying such systems. Stresses the need for accountability and transparency in AI research and practice.

[3] Bommasani, R., Liang, P., & Hashimoto, T. (2022). *Foundation Models in AI: A Technical Overview*.
Summary: Provides a comprehensive technical overview of foundation models like GPT. Explores their applications in various domains and their underlying architectures. Emphasizes transparency and ethical considerations in their development and use.

[4] Bommasani, R., Dai, A. M., & Kaplan, J. (2022). *Foundation Models and Their Socioeconomic Impacts*. Journal of AI Research, **55** (1), 95–115.
Summary: Discusses the socioeconomic impacts of foundation models, including GPT. Examines their transformative potential in business, education, and healthcare. Calls for careful governance to ensure equitable outcomes in AI deployment.

[5] Bubeck, S., Chandrasekaran, V., Eldan, R., et al. (2023). *Sparks of Artificial General Intelligence: Early Experiments with GPT-4*.
Summary: Explores GPT-4's emergent behaviors and generalized intelligence capabilities. Analyzes problem-solving abilities across diverse domains and tasks. Suggests GPT-4 may approach artificial general intelligence (AGI).

[6] Brown, T. B., Mann, B., Ryder, N., et al. (2020). *Language Models Are Few-Shot Learners*. Summary: Advances in Neural Information Processing Systems (NeurIPS), **33**.
Summary: Introduces GPT-3, highlighting its ability to perform tasks with minimal examples. Demonstrates few-shot, one-shot, and zero-shot learning capabilities. Revolutionized NLP by setting new benchmarks for generative AI.

[7] Devlin, J., Chang, M.-W., Lee, K., & Toutanova, K. (2019). *BERT: Pretraining of Deep Bidirectional Transformers for Language Understanding*. Proceedings of the 2019 Conference of the North American Chapter of the Association for Computational Linguistics (NAACL-HLT).
Summary: Introduces BERT, a bidirectional transformer model designed for understanding text. Improves context comprehension in tasks like sentiment analysis and question answering. Revolutionized NLP by enabling pretraining on vast text corpora.

[8] Floridi, L., & Chiriatti, M. (2020). *GPT-3: Its Nature, Scope, Limits, and Consequences*. Minds and Machines, **30** (4), 681–694.
Summary: Examines GPT-3's capabilities, limitations, and ethical implications. Discusses concerns about overreliance on AI in creative and intellectual domains. Advocates for monitoring and regulation of advanced AI systems.

[9] Hendrycks, D., Burns, C., Basart, S., et al. (2021). *Aligning AI with Shared Human Values*. Advances in Neural Information Processing Systems (NeurIPS), **34**.

https://doi.org/10.1515/9783111710808-026

Summary: Proposes strategies to align AI models like GPT with human values. Discusses ethical challenges, including fairness, bias, and accountability. Calls for interdisciplinary collaboration to create responsible AI systems.

[10] Kalyan, K. S., & Sangeetha, S. (2023). *ChatGPT in Academia: Opportunities and Challenges*. Journal of AI Research, **47** (2), 123–140.
Summary: Explores ChatGPT's role in academic research, writing, and education. Highlights opportunities for enhancing learning but warns of plagiarism risks. Calls for guidelines to ensure responsible use of AI in academia.

[11] Li, X., Wu, Y., & Tang, J. (2023). *Large Language Models in Practice: ChatGPT and Beyond*.
Summary: Discusses the practical applications of ChatGPT across various industries. Examines its use cases in customer service, content creation, and education. Explores limitations and areas for future development.

[12] Manning, C. D. (2023). *Generative AI and Large Language Models in 2023: A Survey*. AI Open, **3**, 15–32.
Summary: Surveys the progress of generative AI models like GPT-3 and GPT-4. Highlights advancements, challenges, and ethical considerations. Discusses potential societal and economic impacts of generative AI.

[13] Marcus, G., & Davis, E. (2023). *GPT-4: Power and Pitfalls*. Communications of the ACM, **66** (7), 35–39.
Summary: Critically examines the strengths and weaknesses of GPT-4. Highlights issues with reliability, interpretability, and factual accuracy. Advocates for caution in deploying such powerful AI systems.

[14] OpenAI. (2023). *GPT-4 Technical Report*. OpenAI Research Publication.
Summary: Details the architecture, training, and capabilities of GPT-4. Focuses on advancements in reasoning, contextual understanding, and robustness. Presents use cases and challenges associated with deploying GPT-4.

[15] Radford, A., Wu, J., Amodei, D., et al. (2019). *Language Models are Unsupervised Multitask Learners*. OpenAI Blog, **1** (8), 1–5.
Summary: Introduces GPT-2, highlighting its generative and multitask learning capabilities. Discusses risks of misuse, including generating misleading or harmful content. Pioneered the trend of pre-trained unsupervised language models.

[16] Sheng, E., Chang, K.-W., & Natarajan, P. (2020). *Bias in AI Models: The Case of GPT-2*. Proceedings of the Association for Computational Linguistics (ACL), 101–110.
Summary: Investigates biases present in GPT-2's outputs and their implications. Analyzes how training data contributes to biases in language models. Proposes strategies to mitigate harmful biases in AI systems.

[17] Vaswani, A., Shazeer, N., Parmar, N., et al. (2017). *Attention Is All You Need*. Advances in Neural Information Processing Systems (NeurIPS), **30**.
Summary: Introduces the Transformer architecture, foundational for modern language models. Replaces recurrent layers with self-attention, improving scalability and efficiency. Pioneered breakthroughs in NLP tasks, enabling the development of GPT models.

[18] Wu, X., Yang, Z., & Zhou, S. (2023). *Ethics of AI and ChatGPT: Current Perspectives*. Ethics in AI Research, **12** (4), 223–240.
Summary: Examines ethical issues surrounding the deployment of ChatGPT and similar systems. Focuses on biases, misinformation, and the need for accountability in AI. Proposes frameworks for responsible AI usage and development.

[19] Zhang, Y., Wang, S., He, X., et al. (2023). *ChatGPT: Applications, Opportunities, and Threats*.
Summary: Provides a review of ChatGPT's applications across various fields. Highlights potential threats like misinformation and ethical concerns. Discusses future directions for improving large language models.

[20] Zhang, Y., Sun, K., & He, Q. (2023). *A Comprehensive Study of ChatGPT: Advancements, Limitations, and Future Directions*. Information, **14** (8), 462.
Summary: Explores ChatGPT's architecture, training data, and capabilities. Highlights its advancements in conversational AI and real-world applications. Discusses limitations and areas for further research and improvement.

www.ingramcontent.com/pod-product-compliance
Lightning Source LLC
Chambersburg PA
CBHW071248050326
40690CB00011B/2306